To Sarah —

With high regards

and

Best Wishes!

Rodney

# LEONARDO DA VINCI
# &
# THE GUNS OF COLUMBUS

**The Sole Surviving Gun That Can Be Documented To Da Vinci
Is A Gold & Silver Heraldically Adorned Matchlock Gifted To
Christopher Columbus By Queen Isabella In 1493 –
Making It the Oldest Known American Gun**

# LEONARDO DA VINCI
# &
# THE GUNS OF COLUMBUS

**The Sole Surviving Gun That Can Be Documented To Da Vinci Is A Gold & Silver Heraldically Adorned Matchlock Gifted To Christopher Columbus By Queen Isabella In 1493 – Making It the Oldest Known American Gun**

## Rodney Hilton Brown

The War Museum Press, Ltd

First Edition – Published 2021 by

The War Museum Press
181 Washington Street
Fairhaven, MA 02719

ISBN: 978-1-7334294-6-7 Hardback
ISBN: 978-1-7334294-7-4 Softback

PRINTED IN THE UNITED STATES OF AMERICA

# TABLE OF CONTENTS

# TABLE OF CONTENTS

# TABLE OF CONTENTS

## PART II
## GUNS OF COLUMBUS - ALL TYPES -

## ESTE ES EL FIN

# ACKNOWLEDGEMENTS

Discovering an important relic of history, researching its untold story, and turning it into a book is certainly as hard as it sounds. This 20-year + labor of love was both challenging and often exhausting. So, I especially want to thank the individuals and organizations that helped make this possible.

First and foremost, I would like to express my very deep appreciation to Norman Flayderman. In my young teens, Norm hooked me on collecting arms and armor by giving me an informal "credit line" to buy now and pay later. In my early 20s he published my first book "American Polearms" on condition that it obtain approval by the Review Board of the Company of Military Historians. When he first showed me his gun with Christopher Columbus' motto on it, I told him I had to have it – even though he cautioned that it could not have belonged to Columbus because of the advanced Automatic-Opening-Pan-Cover ignition system that likely post-dated Columbus by a few decades. The little bird on my shoulder told me it was Columbus's personal gun. But I had to make a big leap of faith and gamble on buying it. Buy it I did, and this book is "the rest of the story."

A debt of gratitude is also owed to another of my early mentors, Harold L. Peterson, author of "Arms and Armor in Colonial America" and many other works. Pete also inspired me to write my first book, "American Polearms," and I was honored that he wrote a four-page Introduction for it.

I would like to offer my special thanks to Laurence Claiborne Witten II (of Vinland Map fame) and to his widow, Cora Witten, who provided me with Larry's original notes, purchase records and identity of his own source of the gun. In this regard, thanks also go to Leonardo Lapiccirella for his excellent memory in personally confirming to me the origin of the gun.

I would also like to express my very great appreciation to William Gilkerson who, with the help of Norm Flayderman, wrote about the Columbus gun in his classic work: "Boarders Away II." They both stressed the need for further research about the gun, which this book is the answer to.

Also, Members of Armor and Arms Club, founded by Bashford Dean, first Curator of Arms & Armor of the Metropolitan Museum of Art, are also due credit for expressing their early skepticism regarding the dating of the lock mechanism. They inspired me to do the additional ten years of research that led me to the Leonardo Da Vinci 1491-2 Madrid Codices connection. In a similar manner, members of both The Explorers Club and the Company of Military Historians who also endured my lectures on the "Guns of Columbus" and also encouraged my research, all deserve thanks.

During the planning and development of the research for this work, respectful acknowledgements are due to the great pioneers in the history of Spanish Firearms, James D. Lavin and W. Keith Neal – and to M. L. Brown for his groundbreaking work: "Firearms in Colonial America" -- and to the Internet Blogsite: "Viking Sword" -- all of whom are cited herein.

I would also like to thank the staff of the following institutions and organizations for enabling me to visit them personally and conduct research: National Archives; Library of Congress; Nancy Russell, Archivist, NPS History Collection - National Park Service, Harpers Ferry Center for Media Services, WV; and The Explorers Club for their rare copy of Navarrete (and C. H. Ryan, translator).

Finally, I must thank my line editor, Peter D. Willner, CPA. Also my dachshund puppy, Ginger Spice, whose love and constant companionship inspired my dogged determination to finish this work.

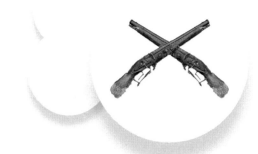

# DEDICATION

This book is respectfully dedicated to:

Leonardo Da Vinci – The Universal Man

Christopher Columbus – The Great Explorer

Queen Isabella of Spain – Por Castilla Y Por Leon Nuevo Mundo Hallo Colon

My father – Linn Patton Brown, Jr., the "Skipper"

And – *"They that go down to the sea in ships, that do business in great waters;*

*These see the works of the Lord, and his wonders in the deep.*

*For he commandeth, and raiseth the stormy wind, which lifteth up the waves thereof.*

*They mount up to the heaven, they go down again to the depths: their soul is melted because of trouble.*

*They reel to and fro, and stagger like a drunken man, and are at their wit's end.*

*Then they cry unto the Lord in their trouble, and he bringeth them out of their distresses.*

*He maketh the storm a calm, so that the waves thereof are still.*

*Then are they glad because they be quiet; so he bringeth them unto their desired haven.*

*Oh that men would praise the Lord for his goodness, and for his wonderful works to the children of men!* [Psalm 107: 23-31 KJV]

# INTRODUCTION

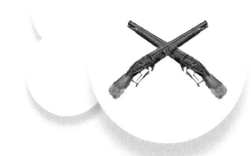

This book, in the making for the last 20 years, is really two books in one:

1. PART I of this book is about the only surviving individual gun that can be documented to Leonardo da Vinci by its unique "instant ignition" AUTOMATIC-OPENING PAN COVER, making it one of the very few of his inventions that were actually made during his lifetime.

2. PART II of the book is about all of the guns used by Columbus when he introduced firearms into the New World. Why bring in Columbus? Because this same only surviving Da Vinci gun is also decorated with gold & silver heraldic adornments and allegorical sculptures that explain its being a gift to Christopher Columbus by Queen Isabella in 1493.

   In sum, this only surviving individual gun that can be documented to da Vinci, is also the one and only surviving gun that can be documented to Christopher Columbus as well.

Da Vinci (1452 – 1519) has long been credited with inventing the wheellock which came into use during his lifetime (early 1500s) and which was illustrated in his CODEX ATLANTICUS.[1]

But, almost a decade earlier than that, da Vinci solved the KEEP YOUR POWDER DRY problem by designing a matchlock with an Automatic-Opening Pan Cover as depicted in his long-lost and recently re-discovered MADRID CODICES (1490-1491), Volume I, Folio 18 v.[2] Although known to have once existed in the 17th Century and cataloged in the Bibliotec National de Madrid, the actual two volumes had vanished from the library shelves and despite several massive searches, were lost for over 200 years. It was assumed they were stolen by French troops during the Napoleonic Wars. But, in 1967 they were accidentally rediscovered by an American musicologist looking for two Medieval song books.

---

1   Vernard L. Foley, Leonardo and the Invention of the Wheellock, Scientific American, January 1988, pages 96-99.

2   The Madrid Codices, Leonardo Da Vinci, McGraw Hill, 1974. By Ladislao Reti. In five volumes with two volumes of Da Vinci's original drawings, transcription translation of Codex Madrid I and transcription translation of Codex Madrid II and a Commentary. The Madrid Codices I–II are in the Biblioteca Nacional de España, with the shelf marks Ms. 8937 and 8936.

Today there is only one sole surviving gun which has this lock ignition mechanism (the Da Vinci-Columbus gun), and this gun is not just similar to the Automatic-Opening Pan Cover as depicted in the MADRID CODICES, but functions exactly the same. It is almost as if the gunsmith had Leonardo and his drawing in the gunsmith shop with him!

Today's firearm historians cannot be blamed for not knowing about the 1491-2 lost MADRID CODICES which show Da Vinci's highly detailed drawings of the Automatic-Opening Pan Cover lock mechanism on the gun. Although the Codices had been discovered in the 1970s, it took several decades for them to be transcribed, translated and published. Then, it took decades more for the information in them to be absorbed into the many specialized areas of the academic world. Even when the United Nations announced the Codicies' finding in Anna Maria Brizio's 1974 article in the UNESCO Courier – no mention of the Matchlock was made!

In dating this gun to the 1490s, we have not only Leonardo's 1491-2 dated MADRID CODICES, but, in addition, the gun is also highly adorned with gold and silver heraldry which, as we will see below, also dates it to 1493. These dual confirmations (Codex depiction + dated heraldry) make the gun pretty much self-authenticating. As a law professor would say: *res ipsa loquitor* (the thing speaks for itself).

"Keeping Your Powder Dry" was not just a rhetorical slogan of the 16th Century, but rather a bitter reminder of a technological problem that had been holding back the development of early firearms for well over a century. The open flashpan of the 13th and 14th centuries was an invitation for wind or rain to blow away or dampen the priming powder just as the burning match was just about to ignite the priming charge in the flashpan and fire the gun.

In this era, firing a "gonne" required two men, one to hold the gun and aim it – and another to put the burning match into the flashpan and ignite the charge. This system was obviously slow, cumbersome and inaccurate. Ironically, it took longer to invent an all-weather ignition system than it did to develop guns in the first place.

In fact, it took the unparalleled genius of the great military inventor LEONARDO DA VINCI to invent two "instant ignition" systems that would allow a single soldier to aim and fire his gun at the same time! In terms of warfare, the invention of the "self-igniting gun" was the 15th century equivalent of inventing the Atomic Bomb in the 20th century. This technological leap changed the course of warfare by enabling more accurate and faster-firing guns. As a result, power on the battlefield shifted away from the Knight-in-Shining-Armor to the relatively easily trained peasant infantryman with his arquebus, or musket.

With its gold and silver decorations, and its chiseled steel sculptural décor, this gun is just as much a work of art as it is a weapon of war. Moreover, in addition to the Automatic-Opening Pan Cover Mechanism having been designed by Da Vinci, much of the gun's artistic décor seems to have his fingerprints all over it. For example, as will be seen below, there are six dragons adorning the gun, and these look to be distinctively Da Vinci-style dragons. Not every renaissance artist made their dragons the same way. Da Vinci's dragons were quite different from his contemporaries, such as Michelangelo's or Albrecht Durer's dragons (as will be shown later).

While it is impossible to know after 500+ years how much of the gun could be attributed to Da Vinci, his students or apprentices, it does seem like an improbable coincidence that the one and only known gun with Da Vinci's unique lock mechanism also is adorned with distinctive and sophisticated artistry that appears in Da Vinci's other works of art.

Finally, it will be seen that the artistic and heraldic décor on the gun actually celebrates two great Spanish victories:

1.  The Conquest of Granada (1492), and

2.  The Conquest of the Sea of Darkness - Discovery of the New World (1492).

As will be seen, Columbus did have guns on his First Voyage, but none have survived to be identified or documented as such. Notwithstanding that this Da Vinci/Columbus Gun is from the Second Voyage, since it is the only surviving gun that can be identified and documented to Christopher Columbus, that appears to make it the oldest known American and/or New World gun.

# PART I

# DA VINCI'S
# GUN FOR COLUMBUS

# THE ROLE OF FIREARMS IN EARLY SPAIN AND THE RECONQUISTA

As noted in the INTRODUCTION, "Keeping Your Powder Dry" was not just a rhetorical slogan of the 16ᵗʰ Century, but rather a bitter reminder of a technological problem that had been holding back the development of early firearms for well over a century.

LEONARDO DA VINCI's invention of his two "instant ignition" systems constitute a technological development which came after centuries of firearms development in Spain:

1.  The pre-existing Matchlock with a tiller-trigger mechanism.
2.  Da Vinci's Matchlock with an Automatic-Opening Pan Cover (MADRID CODICES, 1491).
3.  Da Vinci's Wheellock, circa 1510, (see Da Vinci's CODEX ATLANTICUS),

So, as you will learn below, Da Vinci was definitely the inventor of the Columbus gun's firearm ignition mechanism known as the MATCHLOCK WITH AUTOMATIC-OPENING PAN COVER (MADRID CODICES, 1491). And, his was the first gun in the world to solve the KEEP YOUR POWDER DRY problem. But, what led up to this?

We must first examine the surprisingly early role of firearms in Spain and in the Reconquista.

## FIREARMS IN EARLY SPAIN

EARLY USE OF FIREARMS IN SPAIN: 1118 – 1492. THE BEGINNINGS.

The Spanish Reconquest, or Reconquista, lasted more than seven hundred years. The Moors were finally driven out of Grenada, their last stronghold in Spain, in 1492 during the reign of the Catholic Monarchs, Ferdinand II of Aragon and Queen Isabella of Leon and Castile. Their marriage had united Spain for the first time.

The story of the role of firearms in this epic struggle was well recounted by James D. Lavin in his ground-breaking work, A History of SPANISH FIREARMS:

"Exactly a century and a half earlier, in one battle of the perpetual struggle, Alfonso XI of Castilla laid siege to the then Moorish port of Algeciras. In his account, the royal chronicler tells, for the first time in the history of the Peninsula, how there rained upon the besieging army great balls of iron and "arrows so long and thick that a man could only with great effort raise them from the ground." Hurled by "thunderers" from within the city, they were propelled with such force that many passed overhead and fell harmlessly behind the attacking army."[3]

"[April, 1343] And being very near the city, the Christians went about fully armed day and night, and suffered many casualties: they received many arrow wounds and many stone wounds and many lance wounds: and there were thrown at them many stones from their engines, and many stones of iron which were hurled by thunderers, and of which the soldiers were sorely afraid, for whatever member of a man they touched was carried away as if cut from him by a knife: and however slightly one might be wounded by them, he would soon he dead, for no surgery whatever could save him: firstly because they came burning like fire and also because the powders by which they were launched were of such a nature, that any wound they entered, was mortal; and they flew with such a speed that they would pass through a man fully armed."[4]

As historian Leonard Williams explains:

"The Count of Clonard quotes Pedro Megía's *Silva de Varias Lecciones* to show that gunpowder was known in Spain as early as the eleventh century. "Thunders" of some description seem to have been used at the siege of Zaragoza in 1118; and a Moorish author, writing in 1249, describes in fearsome terms "the horrid noise like thunder, vomiting fire in all directions, destroying everything, reducing everything to ashes." Al-Jattib, the historian of Granada, wrote at the beginning of the fourteenth century that the sultan of that kingdom used at the siege of Baza "a mighty engine, applying fire thereto, prepared with naphtha and with balls." The Chronicle of Alfonso the Eleventh describes in a quaint and graphic passage the crude artillery of that period, and the panic it occasioned."[5]

Almost immediately, this new weapon of war was adopted by the Spanish, most likely the first devices being obtained by capture. As Lavin reports:

The "Trueno or thunderer (thunderclap) remained its common name until the early years of the sixteenth century. By 1359, bombarda, an onomatopoeic word, taken from the Italian,

---

3 Lavin, James D., A History of SPANISH FIREARMS, New York, 1965, page 39. See also, James D. Lavin, "An Examination of Some Early Documents Regarding the Use of Gunpowder in Spain." *Journal of the Arms and Armour Society*, IV (March 1964), pp. 163-9.
4 Ibid. See also, Cayetano Rosell (ed.), *Cronicas de los reyes de Castilla* (Madrid: Imperenta de los Sucesores de Hernando, 1919,), Vol. I, (BAE Vol. 66), page 359. Cronica de Alfonso XI de Castilla.
5 Williams, Leonard, The Arts and Crafts of Older Spain, Chicago, 1908, page 269.

was also used to describe these machines, by then used on shipboard as well as on land.[6] The years preceding the final defeat of the Moors saw the development of a variety of firearms. The Marques de Santillana in his allegorical poem commemorating the naval battle of Ponza (1425) introduces the gun into literature when he fills the air with the "smoky fog" of "rebabdoquines." This was but one of dozens of pieces forming that group of arms already known by the second quarter of the fifteenth century as artilleria, so named, according to Covarrubias, "for the diabolical art of their invention."[7]

Firearms terminology was also as confusing then as it is now. As firearms developed, the terminology overlapped both time periods and the weapons themselves. As Lavin details:

"During the period in which the matchlock was the only 'hand fire-arm, it was known simply as an arcabuz (derived from hacabuche) or escopeta.10 Apparently synonymous with arcabuz in the earliest years of the sixteenth century, escopeta was used exclusively by such writers as Bernal Diaz del Castillo. He, describing the conquest of Mexico (1519-21), mentions arquebusiers or "escopeteros as they were called then," [#11] and makes no reference to the crossbow without including the escopeta. This term early gave way to arcabuz only to reappear during the second half of the seventeenth century when it gradually began to replace arcabuz to indicate an unrifled sporting arm, the meaning it retains today."[8]

With respect to these lighter-weight Spanish firearms, it seems clear that the predecessor of them all was the simple handgun, or "handgonne." The arquebus, musket appears to have been a gun which was introduced about the mid-15th century, following the *hacabuche*, also called the *espingarda*.

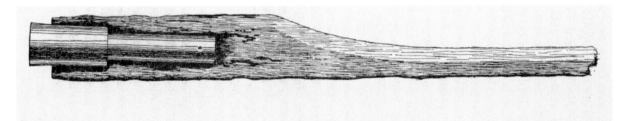

Fig. 2. A fifteenth century Spanish handgun, one of two said to have been brought from Málaga to Madrid in 1831. The powder chamber and barrel are of different calibres (24mm and 41mm respectively); the stock is of oak. Real Armería, Madrid (K.1).

"Even earlier is the handgun K.1 in the Real Armeria (Fig. 2). This has a short iron barrel scarcely two palms long in which the combustion chamber and the receptacle for the projectile are bored separately. The former has a diameter of 2 4mm, while the latter is 4imm. This

---

6   Ibid., page 495.

7   Lavin's page 40 footnotes: <u>Romance antiguo y verdadero de Alora la bien cercada</u> (ca. 1434), "con la gran artilleria—hecho te habia un portillo." S. Griswold Morley (ed.), <u>Spanish Ballads</u> (New York: Henry Holt, 1938), p. 26; and also: Sebastian de Covarrubias, <u>Tesoro de la lengua castellana o espanola</u> (Madrid, 1611), fol. 93V.

8   Levin, page 44, referencing his footnote #11: Bernal Diaz del Castillo, <u>Historia verdadera de la conquista de Nueva Espana</u> (Mexico: Pedro Robredo, 1939), Vol. I, p. 115.

difference is obvious in the step-down construction of the exterior of the barrel. The touch-hole is in the upper centre of the extreme breech. The barrel is mounted upon what appears to be its original stock, an oak pole widened and inletted at its forward end. The widened section is offset slightly to the right, possibly indicating that the extension of the pole was' held under the gunner's left arm, leaving his right hand free to handle the ignition. Whatever device was used to secure the barrel to the stock is now missing. This handgun, together with a companion piece (RAM, K.2), was sent to the Armeria from Málaga in 1831.[9]

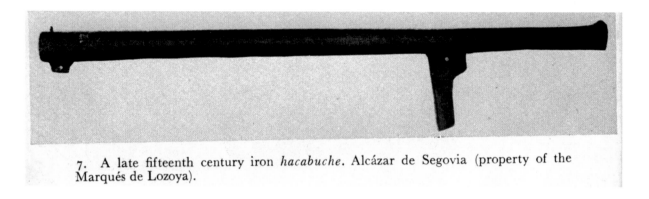

7. A late fifteenth century iron *hacabuche*. Alcázar de Segovia (property of the Marqués de Lozoya).

"Among the earliest handguns surviving in Spain is one belonging to the Marques de Lozoya and on loan to the Alcázar of Segovia (Plate 7).[10] A late fifteenth century piece, although of iron, it is almost undoubtedly a hacabuche. Roughly five palms long, with a 1" bore, it bears a spur on the underside of the barrel towards the muzzle. At the breech, the touchhole (called *fogo* at this date), off centre to the right but well above the side of the barrel, is drilled above an integrally forged flashpan. The lack of any extension beyond the breech and holes through the barrel spur and below the breech make it obvious that this barrel was pin mounted to a wooden stock. Made with no breech plug, the barrel is fitted with iron sights at the muzzle and extreme breech."[11]

Moving along to the Espingarda:

"Alfonso de Palencia says it was employed against the rebels of Toledo in 1467; and the Chronicle of Don Alvaro de Luna relates that when this nobleman was standing beside Don Iñigo d'Estúñiga, upon a certain occasion in 1453, "a man came out in his shirt and set fire to an *espingarda*, discharging the shot thereof above the heads of Don Alvaro and of Iñigo d'Estúñiga, but wounding an esquire."[12]

---

9   Levin, pages 41-43.
10   Lavin, page 54.
11   Ibid
12   Williams, page 272.

"As time advanced, portable firearms of first-rate quality were made throughout the northern Spanish provinces, and also in Navarra, Cataluña, Aragon, and Andalusia. The inventory of the Dukes of Alburquerque mentions, in 1560, "four flint arquebuses of Zaragoza make ... another[273] arquebus of Zaragoza, together with its fuse," and "arquebuses of those that are made within this province" (*i.e.* of Segovia). Cristóbal Frisleva, of Ricla in Aragon, and Micerguillo of Seville were celebrated makers of this arm; but probably these and all the other Spanish masters of this craft derived their skill from foreign teaching, such as that of the brothers Simon and Peter Marckwart (in Spanish the name is spelt *Marcuarte*,) who were brought to Spain by Charles the Fifth."[13]

As Levin well states: "A more ambiguous term is espingarda. Vargas' account is the work of more than one scribe, and at that period when language was more picturesque than exact, it is not surprising that one man's sacabuche was another man's espingardas."[14]

As can be seen from the preceding photo, the early 16th century hacabuche was a monstrous handgun, often measuring over 5ft. and weighing a back-breaking 30-35 pounds! Due to its tremendous weight, it made a great rampart, or wall gun, as well as an infantry gun.

Their heavy barrels were possibly supported by and fired from a fork, although Lavin finds that these forks: "neither appear listed among the equipment of foot soldiers nor depicted in contemporary illustrations prior to the seventeenth century."[15] However, other 16th and 17th century European sources show the contemporary and abundant use of forks (see Maximillian Codex illustrations, etc.)

---

13   Ibid.
14   Levin, page 43.
15   Ibid., page 44, referencing his footnote #12: Bernal Diaz del Castillo, *Historia verdadera de la conquista de Nueva Espana* (Mexico: Pedro Robredo, 1939), Vol. I, p.i 15. "According to an inspection of the* garrison of St, Augustine, Florida^ made on 27 September, 1578, the equipmentofanarcabucero consisted of an arquebus, sword, powder flask, and charges. Jeanette Thurber Conner (ed. and trans.), GolomatJ Records of Spanish Florida (Delarid: The Florida State Historical Society, 1930), Vol. II, p. 136.

## Illustration credit: Bashford Dean

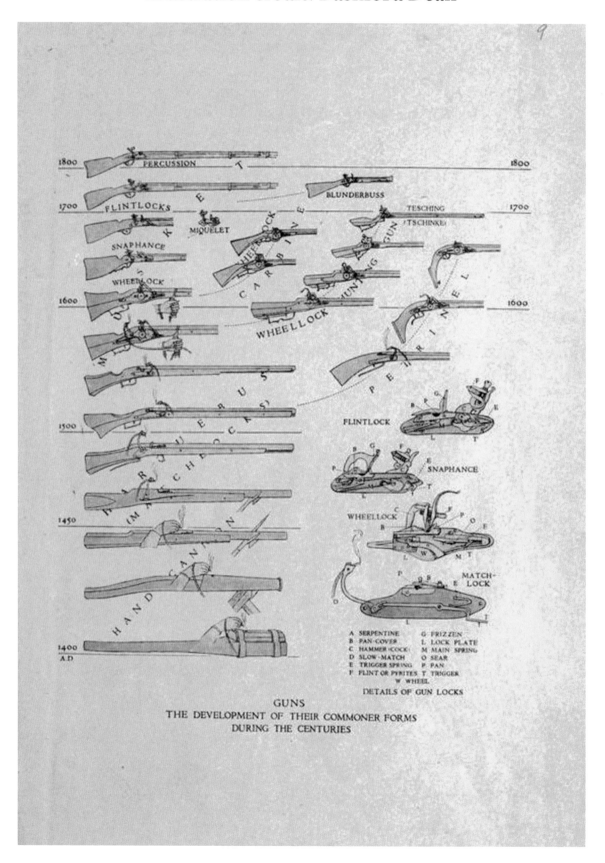

## INVENTION OF THE MATCHLOCK

The next important step in the development of the firearm was the invention of an ignition mechanism that would hold the lighted match chord and guide it down into the flashpan. This mechanism started out as a wrought iron lever with a small vice on the top end that would hold the burning match. At first, this lever was simply attached to the side of the gun with a screw in the middle. Later, in the 15th century, a metal plate affixed to the side of the gun held the lever, resulting in the invention of the first gun lock.[16]

## Illustration courtesy of CLEPHAN

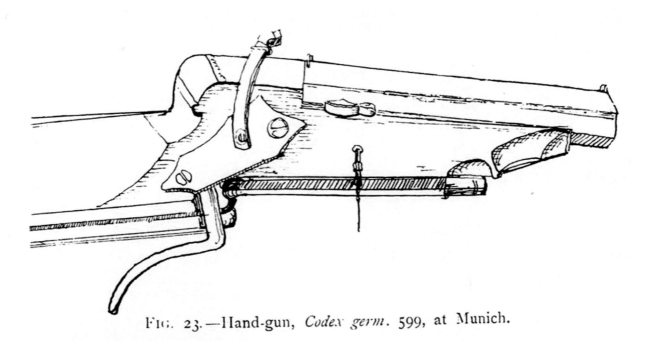

FIG. 23.—Hand-gun, *Codex germ.* 599, at Munich.

These new locks were of the so-called "sear type" with only two moving parts: the serpentine and the sear. The serpentine and the sear (and the stationary sear spring) were attached to the rectangular lockplate which, as stated above, was mounted flush with the stock and fastened from the sideplate (opposite the lockplate) by two bolts. The "tiller trigger," or operating lever was screwed into the bottom surface of the long, rocking sear.

Like some of the hacabuche and espingardas before them, the matchlock's flash pan was rectangular and welded to the right-hand side of the breech. In addition, a horizontally swinging, hand-operated pancover was added in an attempt to keep the priming powder dry, and also enabled the piece to be primed in advance. However, this improvement still didn't render the gun completely weatherproof.

---

16   Ibid., pages 43-44.

Another curious and impracticable form of serpentine is illustrated in Codex MS. 1, 390, in the University Library at Erlangen, a record dating in the second half of the fifteenth century.[17]

Fig. 22.—Harquebusier, *temps* Maximilian I.

**A Maximillian I Harquebusier, ca. 1480–1510.[18]**

17   ROBERT COLTMAN CLEPHAN, F.S.A., <u>AN OUTLINE OF THE HISTORY AND DEVELOPMENT OF HAND FIREARMS, FROM THE EARLIEST PERIOD TO ABOUT THE END OF THE FIFTEENTH CENTURY</u>, New York, 1906, page 62.

18   Ibid., page 63. Another early example of this form occurs in Codex Germanicus 734, a MS. in the Royal Library at Munich dating in the third quarter of the fifteenth century. Note: The Cgm 558, or *Codex Germanicus Monacensis*, is a convolution of two 15th-century manuscripts with a total of 176 folia, bound together in the 16th century. It is kept at the Bavarian library in Munich.

**A rack of Maximillian I Harquebuses and a pair of Harquebusiers pictured in the famous "Maximilian" arsenal books (German: *Maximilianische Zeugbücher*, also referred to as *"cod. icon"*), illustrated by Jörg Kölderer ca. 1495-1515, (see fol. 114, and also *'Messing hagkennpuchsen'* (wall guns with brass barrels) respectively, and fol. 131 and 132, both in *cod. icon. 222*.[19]**

---

19   While there are numerous sources for digital copies of the Maximillian Arsenal Books, the best selection focusing on harquebuses is a brilliant monograph appearing in www.vikingsword.com , the Ethnographic Arms & Armour Forum: *"Ca. 1520: One of the World's Oldest and Finest Matchlock Landsknecht Arquebuses,"* Posted by Michael on 19th May 2014. See: http://www. vikingsword.com/vb/showthread.php?t=18532&highlight=haquebut+graz+hofkircher. See also: *Codex Monacensis* for additional illustrations of Maximillian I's Arsenal done by the artist Nicolaus Glockenthon in 1505. Some of the weapons illustrated are "hand gonnes," and one appears to be a snapping matchlock. However, most appear to have a simple gravity-operated serpentine falling towards the shooter and controlled by the fingers of the left hand wrapped under the barrel.

12. A Catalán militiaman of 1641 with his arquebus and fork. On his belt are hung extra matches, flask and charges. Llibre de passantia, Gremio de los plateros de Barcelona.

**Illustration in Lavin of a Catalonian harquebusier of the 1600s. However, due to the Spanish tradition of extended use of firearms beyond their technological "expiration date," this illustration also represents harquebusiers for the previous century and a half as well.[20]**

---

20　Lavin, page 58, plate 12.

As Lavin reports:

"As late as 1646, when the matchlock was still extensively used by the Spanish military (Plate 12), they were made useless by inclement weather as when on 22 November of that year, during the battle of Lerida, 'There blew such a furious and cold wind that it tumbled us from our horses; it was much feared that it would hinder us for it snatched the powder the moment the pans were uncovered making it impossible to fire.'"[21]

---

21   Ibid., page 45, referencing: Baltasar Gracian y Morales, *La relation graciana sobre el socorro de LSrida*, Ms. 959 (K.3.20^, ff. 325r-328v, Trinity College, Dublin.

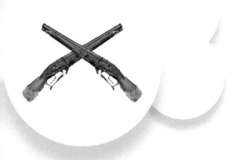

# THE GUNS AT GRENADA

## TRANSFORMING & MODERNIZING THE SPANISH ARMY

The Spanish military was completely transformed during the reign of Ferdinand and Isabella. During this time its weaponry, tactics, training and mode of recruitment was "modernized." As described by Jean Hippolyte Mariejol and David Nicolle:

"The war against Affonso V of Portugal (1474 to 1476) was a struggle that recalls the melees of the Middle Ages; but at the death of the Catholic Sovereigns Spain possessed a truly modern army, composed chiefly of infantry and relying not so much on individual bravery as on the solidity of its battalions, the agility of its movements, and the skill of its leaders."[22]

"For several centuries, the Kingdom of Castile had been somewhat isolated, technologically, from the rest of Europe, although this was changing by the late 15th century. Aragon, however, had been more outwardly reaching, due to its Catalonian ports on the Mediterranean Sea. By the close of the 15th century, the arms and armour of their respective military elites were virtually identical and modernized under a unified command structure."[23]

Mariejol well-illustrates the structure of these feudal military obligations:

"To judge the importance and value of the new organization, we must picture to ourselves the feudal rout of the early days of the reign. When the sovereigns were menaced by a Portuguese invasion, or when they prepared to make an incursion into Moslem territory, they summoned their vassals to arms. The contingents of the nobility and the towns began to gather. The number of troops raised by each lord varied according to his territorial wealth and importance. Sometimes a noble commanded in person; often he placed some captain of renown at the head of his troops. The crown lands furnished levies that were led in combat by adelantados or other royal officers. The cities and towns sent their men under the orders of captains or of

22   Jean Hippolyte Mariejol (Translated and Edited by Benjamin Keen), The SPAIN of Ferdinand and Isabella, New Brunswick, New Jersey. Rutgers University Press, 1961, Page 192.
23   David Nicolle, PhD - GRANADA 1492, Osprey Military, 1998.

corregidores. These municipal militias, like the royal and seigniorial forces, included foot soldiers and horsemen, nobles and commoners. In the Spanish communes the obligation of personal service was so imperative for the nobility that a caballero who could not furnish arms and a horse was reduced to the condition of a taxpayer (pacer). He must be able to show the public registrar and swear on the Cross that he possessed 'sword, lance, shield, cuisses, morion, and cuirass, and, of course, a war horse.'"[24]

# THE NEW ARTILLERY – THE THUNDER OF GOD

Although the ultimate strength of the army came to reside in its infantry, it was the artillery to whom the Sovereigns were indebted for the conquest of Granada:

"Historians have not sufficiently noted the decisive role of the artillery in the last struggle against the Moslems. The War of Granada was above all one of sieges, with large-scale battles of secondary importance; the towns were taken one by one, and when Granada was isolated, it fell of itself."[25]

> "At the start of the war, Isabella summoned blacksmiths and engineers from Italy, Flanders, and Germany; she imported considerable quantities of gunpowder from Sicily and Portugal; she assembled a powerful artillery, composed of pieces of varying caliber and types: "*lombardas, pasabolantes, cabratanas, ribadoqulnes,* and *buzanes.*" The great lombards were regarded as particularly terrible. Yet these instruments of destruction, as Prescott remarks, were very crude."[26]

> "The service of the artillery involved a multitude of secondary services. "To make munitions and equipment of the artillery, there were employed many blacksmiths, carpenters, sawyers, woodcutters, smelters, masons, stone-cutters who looked for stone quarries, and other stone-cutters who worked the stone, and diggers, charcoal-burners whose job it was to make charcoal for the forges, and esparteros who made ropes and baskets. And over each group of workers was an overseer (ministro) who urged on the workers and supplied them with the things they needed for their task."[27]

---

24   Mariejol, page 193.
25   Ibid., page 199.
26   Ibid., page 200.
27   Ibid. See also: Luis Ribot García, "Types of Armies: Early Modern Spain," in *War and Competition Between States*, ed. Philippe Contamine (New York: Oxford University Press, 2000), 47.

**1548 Print showing a lombard by Johan Petretus entitled "Nemlichen des aller namhafftigisten hochersarnesten/Rominschen Architection," Nurnberg. Collection of the author.**

"The pieces [artillery] were [operated by and] serviced not by Spaniards but by Germans, more skilled in the use of these machines of war;"[28]

"All this proves that the Catholic Sovereigns were fully aware of the importance of the new arm. It is equally clear that the conquest of Granada was due less to the bravery of the feudal chivalry than to these fearful engines of destruction. No wall, however massive, could withstand a sustained fire. Without artillery, the struggle would have dragged on forever or would have come to nothing."[29]

## THE CONQUEST OF GRENADA WAS A HOLY WAR – A RELIGIOUS CRUSADE

The aid of the Pope and the Holy Roman Catholic Church made the conquest of Granada possible. The war was waged as a Holy War – a religious crusade, culminating an almost 800 year *Reconquista*:

---

28    Ibid., page 202.
29    Ibid., page 203.

"The surrender of the city of Granada to Ferdinand of Aragon and Isabella of Castile on 2 January 1492, marked the end of over seven centuries of Muslim political rule in southern Iberia and the culmination of a *Reconquista* movement that was almost equal in duration."[30]

"The imperative to drive the Muslims from these lost territories was seen as God's will, as sentiments of religious and territorial ambition became one and the same."[31]

# FINANCING THE GUNS – THE GIFT OF THE HOLY SEE

The conquest of Granada was financed by the subsidization of the crusade by the Holy See. This financing allowed the Spanish army to buy the newest military technology known at the time:[32]

"The crusade provided Ferdinand and Isabella the funds they needed to build a modern standing army, a common enemy to unify their subjects against, and eventually, the lands of Granada itself. After the conquest of Granada, Spain emerged on the international sphere by funding exploration of North America as well as challenging France militarily in the Italian Wars of the early sixteenth century.[33] None of these developments could have occurred without the benefit of church financing for the crusade against Granada."[34]

Scholars agree that only the wealthiest governments could afford to acquire the gunpowder siege equipment necessary to wage an offensive siege campaign. While "acquisition costs and logistical support for a viable siege artillery train were beyond the means of the feudal lord, or even of a small country like Castile or Aragon alone, papal aid for the crusade subsidized Spanish acquisition of a large artillery force that rivaled that of France or the Ottoman Empire.[35]

A series of Papal bulls provided the capital that Isabella was able to solicit from the Vatican in support of the war, allowed the monarchs to modernize their army to engage in wars of conquest:[36]

---

30   Clark, James, "Florins, Faith and Falconetes in the War for Granada, 1482-92" (2011). *University of Colorado Boulder, Undergraduate Honors Theses.* Paper # 721, page 4.

31   John Edwards, "*Reconquista* and Crusade in Fifteenth-Century Spain," in *Crusading in the Fifteenth Century*, ed. Norman Housley (New York: Palgrave Macmillan, 2004), 165.

32   Weston F. Cook, "The Cannon Conquest of Nasrid Spain and the End of the Reconquista," 43-70. Journal of Military History 57, 1993.

33   Albert D. McJoynt, introduction to *The Art of War in Spain: The Conquest of Granada, 1481-1492*, by William H. Prescott (London: Greenhill Books, 1995), 15-16.

34   Clark, page 5.

35   McJoynt, introduction, 27.

36   Clark, page 10.

"The Papal Bull of 1482 was far more generous to the Spanish monarchs than previous arrangements had been.[37] The bull offers the traditional plenary indulgences, but greatly broadens the participants in the crusade, and in particular the revenue base of the crusade, by offering those indulgences not only to combatants but also to financial contributors who donated at least two silver *reales*.[38] Pope Sixtus IV acknowledged the aims and costs of the crusade in the text of the bull:

> "Our most dear son in Christ the illustrious king Ferdinand, and our most dear daughter Isabella, the queen of Castile and Leon, have begun, partly by our persuasion, to conquer the kingdom of Granada, which the perfidious Saracens occupy. They firmly hope and trust that, God helping, and all the Spanish kingdoms now being at peace, they may be able to achieve the longed-for victory and conquest of the kingdom of Granada which their predecessors sought with such zeal, with the conversion of at least some of the Saracens to the Catholic faith, and with the permanent release and liberation from [Saracen] aggression of the inhabitants of those Christian communities which border on the kingdom. We are conscious that the resources of the king and queen are insufficient for operations against the kingdom of Granada and for such a great exaltation of the faith..."[39]

As the King took command of the troops in the field, Queen Isabella acted as a modern day Quartermaster General. She paid for the vast quantity of arms, supplies and provisions for their army. She was also in charge of organizing horse-drawn trains of armored ambulances. She personally tended to their wounded warriors on the battlefield. In addition to her devout religious fervor, this was why the army and the people of Spain loved her. Isabella risked her life on the battlefields with them, once almost losing her life when her tents were lit on fire by Moorish artillery.

## ISABELLA'S ROLE IN MODERNIZING THE SPANISH ARMY

Isabella ranked among Medieval Spain's intelligentsia. She was well-schooled and literate in an age when not only very few women, but very few in the population (outside of the clergy), could even read or write, or understand mathematics. In addition to being the chief liaison with the Papacy in procuring funds for the war, she also led the effort to recruit the most up-to-date weaponry and skilled gunpowder technicians from all over Europe. Was Leonardo Da Vinci one of those imported weaponry technicians? This possibility will be explored later.

---

37  José Goñi Gaztambide, "The Holy See and the Reconquest of the Kingdom of Granada," in *Spain in the Fifteenth Century*, ed. Roger Highfield (London: The Macmillan Press Ltd, 1972), page 357.

38  Ibid., page 358.

39  Pope Sixtus IV, "Pope Sixtus IV grants the *cruzada* to Ferdinand and Isabella for the war against Granada, 10 August 1482," in *Documents on the Later Crusades, 1274-1580*, ed. Norman Housley (New York: St. Martin's Press, 1996), 156-57.

As David Nicolle ably details:

"It was, however, Queen Isabella who really encouraged a widespread adoption of firearms late in the 15th century, bringing in experts from France, Germany and Italy. Firearms made a decisive impact during the conquest of Granada, not only forming part of a royal artillery train of bronze and iron cannon but also in the form of numerous espingarda handguns. Of course the Muslims had firearms, including espingardas and ribaudequins, but they were few in number. These were used at Moclin in 1486 and at Malaga a year later, but only played a significant role in the final struggle for Granada. This city's defences had, in fact, been strengthened with low semi-circular artillery bastions at the base of some high towers. Yet it might still be true to say that, in the end, the last Andalusian kingdom of Granada was betrayed not by its defenders, nor even its last unfortunate king, Boabdil El Zogoiby —'The Unlucky'— but by its lack of modern gunpowder artillery."[40]

Hernando del Pulgar described the chaos that the Spanish guns caused among the defenders of Ronda in 1485: "in one place the cannon knocked down the wall and in another wrecked the houses and, if they tried to repair the damage made by the *lombardas* they could not, for the unending hail of fire from smaller weapons killed anybody on the walls."[41] The system of mutually supporting fire between different classes of guns kept defenders from repairing breaches or sallying forth to meet the besieging force, and closely resembled the tactics used by the forces of Charles VII in France.[42]

# THE QUEENS GUNS AT GRANADA, 1492: ESPINGARDAS

After Ferdinand and Isabella had recruited a vast number of troops and had also built an efficient command structure, they equipped their army with the latest and best:

"Spanish infantry quickly became associated with the use of handguns in combat because they were purchasable *en masse*. The introduction of the arquebus by the middle of the fifteenth century made handguns viable infantry weapons, because they could now be fired by just one man."[43] "The Spanish were early adopters of the *espingarda*, a particular version of the

---

40 El Cid and the Reconquista 1050-1492, by David Nicolle, Illustrated by Angus McBride. 1988. OSPREY - Men-at-Arms 200 Series, Pages 40 – 41

41 Cook, "The Cannon Conquest of Nasrid Spain," page 63.

42 The Vabanesque system of siegecraft employed in France during the Hundred Years' War called for a sophisticated complementary deployment of guns. According to chronicler Guillaume Leseur, at the siege of Dax French forces first dug trenches and fortifications to protect gunnery crews from defensive fire. Once ready, "the large artillery was fired assiduously day and night. Inside of a few days it had done great damage, so that the defenses of the towers…and a great part of the forward walls were thrown down to the ground; and our said artillery made large and wide breaches there, over which watch was held; and we fired the large culverines at these, so that, when the enemy wished to make shelters or otherwise repair them, our culverines often killed and wounded their men and knocked them down to the ground, them and their shelters." See Clifford J. Rogers, "Military revolutions," 266-67.

43 McJoynt, introduction, page 35.

arquebus. Handguns in the late fifteenth century slightly underperformed crossbows in accuracy and reloading rate, however their "principal advantage was to equip a rapidly expanding infantry army."[44] "Ferdinand swelled his forces by requiring quotas of armed *espingaderos* from the towns. While handguns certainly could not compare to the premier individual missile weapon of the day, the longbow, they could be mass-produced and unskilled urban levies could rapidly achieve proficiency in their use. Longbows on the other hand required master craftsmanship and a lifetime of training to gain proficiency. Longbowmen were supplanted by gunpowder infantry on European battlefields because simply not enough could be fielded to fight continual wars of expansion."[45] In the face of tens of thousands of infantrymen, longbows did not become obsolete, they became irrelevant.

"Just like innovations in gunpowder artillery changed the nature of siege warfare, the preponderance of infantry in early modern armies revolutionized field engagements. Use of the longbow, crossbow, handguns and pikes gave infantry the ability to defeat cavalry and win battles of their own accord."

With the fall of Granada, King Ferdinand and Queen Isabella became world-class heroes, both to their own people, and across the entire Christian World. Grenada was the greatest Christian victory since the disastrous fall of Constantinople in 1453. The glory was shared with God:

"It was His will that the monarchs followed when they rushed to defend Alhama in 1482, and they believed that their diligent service to God allowed them to conquer Granada when none of their predecessors had been able to. Ferdinand and Isabella's subjects followed their pious sovereigns into battle under the banner of crusade in unprecedented numbers. Success was perceived as proof of divine approval, and Ferdinand was able to maintain the impetus of his conquest into further international forays."

"The final conquest of Granada may have reflected divine pleasure with the Catholic monarchs; it certainly reflected their aggressive adoption of the most modern military equipment and techniques available in Europe at the time. Ferdinand brought an army of conquest into the field the likes of which had never been seen in Iberia. It was massive, comprised primarily of infantry, and relied on gunpowder artillery to assault fortified defensive positions. Ferdinand's infantry became a regular standing force of sorts, and they became ruthlessly efficient with both artillery and smaller handguns."[46]

---

44   Ibid., page 36.
45   Ibid., page 37.
46   Clark, page 49.

# WHAT HAPPENED TO THE GUNS OF GRENADA AND THE MANY THOUSANDS OF FIREARMS USED IN THE SPANISH RECONQUISTA?

James Lavin's book amply documents with numerous contemporary references the use of perhaps 10,000 to 20,000 arquebuses during Ferdinand and Isabella's 10-year Conquest of Granada from 1481 to 1492 A.D. What happened to them? They should be all over the place! Where are they now? How can we explain the near complete absence of them in Spanish and other European museums?

A primary explanation for their infinitesimal survival rate was simply their hard use. The Spanish had the frugal habit of re-issuing and re-using these early firearms until they literally fell apart. A good example of this is the poor matchlock arquebus illustrated in a later chapter which dates from the end of the 15th century. It was used in the 15th, 16th, 17th century and in the 18th century its barrel was cut down and the end of the hexagonal barrel was rounded down to take an 18th century triangular-style socket bayonet! It surfaced in Florida near St. Augustine in the 20th century and was immediately acquired by the author.

Another reason is the lack of appreciation the Spanish had for these simple and sometimes crude weapons. The Spanish did not actually form their first national arms and armor collection until after the reign of Carlos V (1516 - 1558).[47] This museum, the Real Armeria, was founded in about 1562, approximately 70 years after fall of Granada. This collection started with Carlos V's personal armor and guns of the wheellock period.

As Lavin describes:

> "The Real Armeria in Madrid houses the world's finest collection of Spanish arms and armour, a collection kept virtually intact since the reign of Carlos V, and enlarged by successive monarchs. Its various inventories form a valuable corpus of evidence.
>
> The first, the Relación de Valladolid, is an inventory of the emperor's arms compiled in 1560, two years after Carlos' death. Transported to Madrid after 1561, this collection formed the nucleus of the Real Armeria. Only twenty-seven firearms, representing the accumulation of more than thirty years, are listed in the inventory. Included are the oldest self-igniting hand firearms [wheellocks, not matchlocks] brought to Spain. The descriptions are brief and it is impossible to identify any existing firearms."[48]

A further reason for the scarcity of these early Spanish guns lies in the French invasion of Spain in 1808 during the Napoleonic wars. On May 2nd of that year [1808], the populace of Madrid rose up against the French invaders and in their search for weapons they broke into the Real Madrid

---

47   Charles *V* (24 February 1500 – 21 September 1558) was Holy Roman Emperor and Archduke of Austria from 1519, King of *Spain* (Castile and Aragon) from 1516, and Lord of the Netherlands as titular Duke of Burgundy from 1506.
48   Lavin, page 27.

armory and looted a significant portion of the collection.[49] However, their uprising failed and the French remained in control.

To make matters even worse, in 1811, three years later, the French-installed King of Spain, Joseph Bonaparte, gave a ball in the great hall of the Real Armeria armory. In order to have room for a dance floor and dinner tables for all the guests, the arms and armor collection (except presumably those hung upon the walls) were moved out and taken into storage. This obviously reduced the collection to a hopeless morass. During the reign of Joseph Bonaparte a further and substantial number of items disappeared from the armory together with other classic works of art and found their way to England where they were auctioned at Christie's in London on 23 and 24 January 1839 and on 24 February 1840.[50]

Finally, the *coupe de gras* came during the Spanish Civil War (1936-39). At that time, the Nationalists under Gen. Francisco Franco decreed that possession of any firearm was an offence punishable by death. Consequently, the owners of many fine and rare pieces destroyed them. That caused the disappearance of a great number of Spain's antique firearms.[51]

This, together with the explanations listed above, accounts for the extreme rarity of Reconquista period Spanish firearms now in Spain outside of a few public museum collections.

---

49  Ibid., page 28.
50  Ibid.
51  Ibid., pages 37 – 38.

# THE DA VINCI GUN PRESENTED TO COLUMBUS BY QUEEN ISABELLA

**The unique, never-before-seen AUTOMATIC-OPENING PAN COVER mechanism
on the "Columbus" matchlock was personally designed by Leonardo da Vinci.
The proof of this is the recent discovery of the lost Madrid Codices of da Vinci which
picture the exact same instant ignition device, and which are dated 1490-1491.**

This gun presented by the Spanish monarchs to Columbus is also the only surviving individual gun that can be specifically documented to Leonardo da Vinci.

Double Confirmation of the Date of Manufacture: In addition to having its unique automatic-opening pan cover lock mechanism illustrated in Leonardo's MADRID CODICES dated 1491, as you will see in the next chapters, the gun is also highly adorned with gold and silver royal Spanish heraldry which also dates it to 1493.

## INSTANT IGNITION AND THE AUTOMATIC-OPENING PAN COVER

Da Vinci has long been credited with inventing the wheellock ignition mechanism, which also came into use during his lifetime (in the early 1500s), about a decade later than the Columbus gun. Due to the infinitesimal survival rate of dated guns of the 15th and early 16th centuries, it is impossible to identify or document any individual wheellock gun to Da Vinci; however, Da Vinci does get credit for inventing that class of firearm.[52]

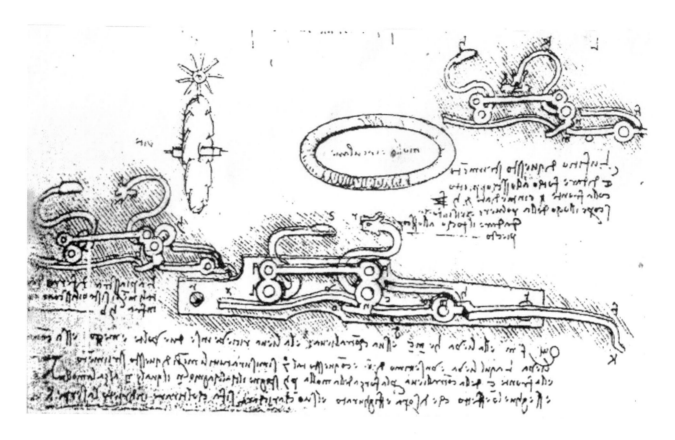

This rare original drawing above of an "automatic-opening" match lock pan cover design was found in the long-lost Madrid Codices, Volume I, Folio 18 v. Although known to have once existed in the 17th Century and cataloged in the Bibliotec National de Madrid, the actual 2 volumes had vanished from the library shelves and despite several massive searches, were lost for over 200 years. They were accidentally rediscovered in 1967. Consequently, they were untranslated and unpublished until relatively recently and this author is not aware of their mention in any recent publications about early firearms history.

How it works (in this author's words): Leonardo invented or designed this "automatic" (his word was "immediate") matchlock ignition system with a rotating tumbler (to which the serpentine, or hammer, was affixed). The tumbler was initially held in place by a sear (latch) of vertical motion. The serpentine was set in motion by squeezing the "tiller-trigger," or operating lever, which pulled back the sear and allowed the tumbler to spin. The tumbler was powered-by a spring which immediately allowed the serpentine to move forward, down into the flashpan and ignite the priming gunpowder. Simultaneously, via a connecting horizontal armature, the fall of the serpentine automatically uncovered the flashpan, exposing the priming powder. This "tiller trigger," or operating

---

52    Vernard L. Foley, Leonardo and the Invention of the Wheellock, Scientific American, January 1988, pages 96-99.

lever, as shown in the drawing above is similar to those found on contemporary Medieval cross-bows and arquebuses.[53]

When releasing the tiller trigger, the serpentine retreats, and the spring simultaneously closes the pan cover. Leonardo's drawings are sufficiently clear and explicit. The design of his mechanism and its operation is not just similar to the Columbus gun -- it is exactly the same.

How it works In Leonardo's Words (Translation of Leonardo's text):

"The purpose of this instrument
is to fire the arquebus with [as the]
front [g]. Immediately, [h] opens the
site of the gunpowder, which is then ignited."[54]

"Here, [f m] is the lever and [m c] is its counterlever. The lever is two and one-half times longer than the counterlever; the lever measures one-seventh of a braccio, and this seventh shall be used for proportioning all of the parts of this instrument. Front [c] of the counterlever, by the force of spring [p h], pushes heel [n] which, in turn, raises spring [v X], causing the effect depicted above to take place. To wind it up, the serpentine [K] must be drawn back to [L]."[55]

## This enlargement shows the pan cover opened and the serpentine descending.

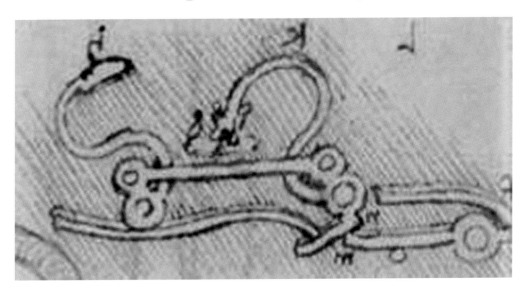

---

53 This "tiller trigger" lever eventually gave way to the short vertical trigger that would be used later in the snaphaunce locks of different origins (Netherlands, Arabic, Germanic and Italic or "a la florentina").

54 In this translation, "[g]" means the Pan Cover, and "[h]" means the Flashpan, i.e. "the site of the gunpowder."

55 The Madrid Codices, Leonardo Da Vinci, McGraw Hill, 1974 By Ladislao Reti. In five volumes with two volumes of Da Vinci's original drawings, transcription translation of Codex Madrid I and transcription translation of Codex Madrid II and a Commentary. 18 VERSO, Page 48, Volume IV.

# COMPARISON OF DA VINCI DRAWING WITH COLUMBUS GUN LOCK

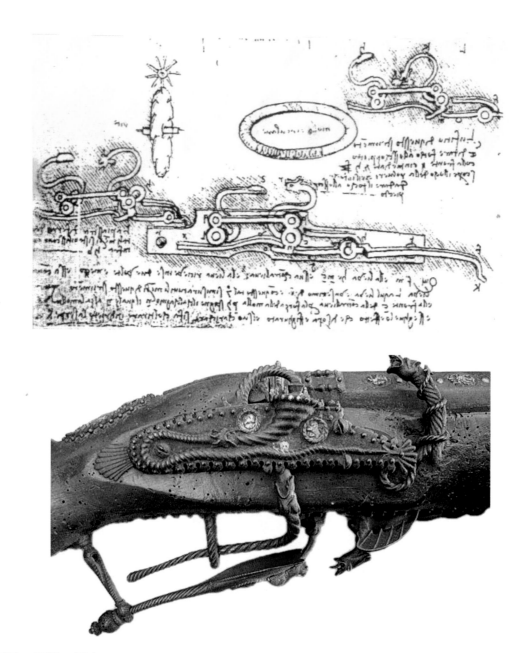

**TT = Tiller Trigger. PC = Pan Cover. SMH = Serpentine Match Holder/Hammer.**

MOVING PARTS: 1. The Da Vinci diagram shows the lock looking at it from the inside (i.e. as if the lock is removed from the gun). The photo of the actual Columbus gun lock shows the lock from the outside, so you only see the upper parts of the Pan Cover and hammer/Serpentine Match Holder (SMH) which stick up from the inside above the lock plate! 2. Also, for reasons unknown, 15th and 16th century gunsmiths generally preferred to have the hammer (SMH) falling back to the rear (toward the shooter's face). So when this gunsmith [presumably] got Da Vinci's diagram, it was an easy fix the turn the tiller trigger around, so the Serpentine Match Holder/Hammer would be falling back.

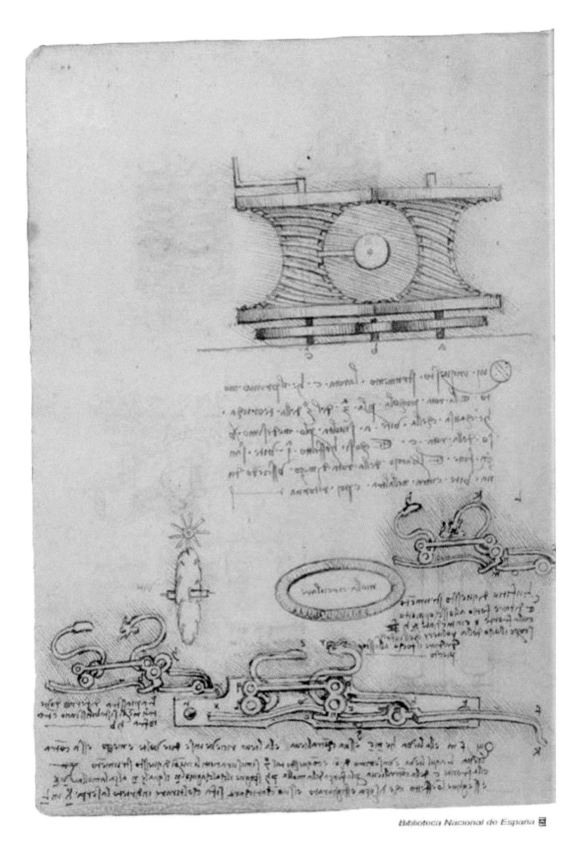

**The entire page which shows the Matchlock design.**
**The Madrid Library's Cover Pages of the Madrid Codices Folios**

*Tratados varios de Fortificacion Estatica y Geometria Escritos en Italiano*

*Por los Años de 1491 como se ve à la vuelta del fol. 157.*

*Advirtiendo que la Letra de este Libro está al reves*

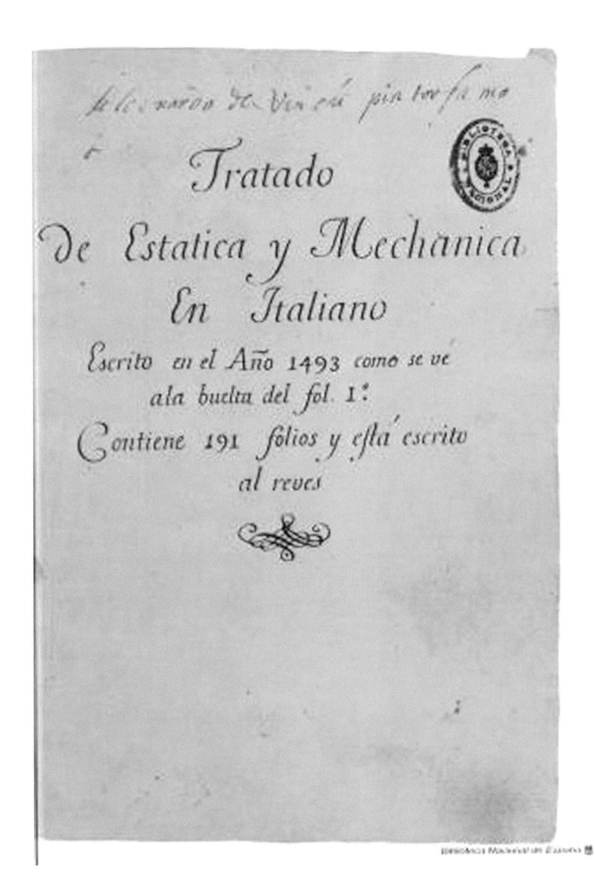

Leonardo da Vinci pintor famoso

Tratado

De Estatica y Mechanica

En Italiano

Escrito en el Año 1493 como se ve
ala buelta del fol. 1º
Contiene 191 folios y esta escrito
al reves

# LEONARDO DA VINCI &
# THE GUN OF COLUMBUS

The Great Explorer has been generally depicted in history as a venturesome sailor with a compass, an astrolabe and a dream. But the man with a dream was also a man with a gun. In fact, lots of them! This book is the first comprehensive explanation of the guns and cannons used on his four voyages and battles with the indigenous Carib and Taino Indians – in essence, the first guns fired in the New World. This book covers the full range of all types of guns and cannon carried on the four voyages. One of Columbus' breech-loading verso cannons excavated from the Jaina River is pictured. However, the highlight of the book is an exciting new discovery, a heraldically gold & silver adorned matchlock Espingole (swivel gun) that some believe to be the personal gun of Christopher Columbus presented to him by Queen Isabella in the spring of 1493.

But as to the gun itself, the author recalls an ancient legal maxim. "Res ipsa loquitur" is an ancient Latin phrase which means: "The thing speaks for itself." In tort law, it is a principle that allows plaintiffs to meet their burden of proof with what is, in effect, clear and overwhelming circumstantial evidence. The plaintiff can create a presumption of proof in the absence of any evidence to the contrary. By applying this doctrine to the evidence regarding the Columbus gun, the words of Leonardo Da Vinci himself come to mind:

> "There are three sorts of people: Those who see, those who see when they are shown and those who do not see."[56]

You, the reader, will make up your own mind based on the evidence that follows.

## COLUMBUS' GUN/ESPINGOLE – PRESENTED IN 1493

Why the spring of 1493? The answer lies in the history of Columbus' relationship with the Catholic Monarchs. Columbus would not have been given such a lavish gift as this gun before his first

---

56   See: www.leonardodavinci.net/quotes.jsp, page 1.

voyage because many in Spain thought he was on a fool's errand. He would sail over the edge of the earth and never be seen nor heard of again. In addition, royal funds were scarce after the expensive campaign to take Granada, and the 1st voyage was frugally provisioned.

The period between Columbus' return from his 1st Voyage and setting sail for his less successful 2nd Voyage was the zenith of Columbus' career. Lavish gifts were bestowed upon him during these months, including a Parchment from Pope Alexander VI presenting Columbus with a piece of the "True Cross." This book cites records from The Archives of the Indies that show Queen Isabella bestowed upon Columbus many types of finery of which the Espingole is just one example. And, other evidence points to the gun as having been presented to the Great Explorer for his Second Voyage by the Queen he loved so dearly.

Always being stabbed in the back by jealous nobles at the Royal Court, when Columbus returned from his 2nd, 3rd and 4th voyages, he was actually accused of not having found "enough" gold, plus, he wasn't Spanish. But in the spring of 1493, it was for a short time, "All Hail to Columbus!"

## COLUMBUS' TRIUMPHANT RETURN, RECEPTION AND HONORS IN BARCELONA, APRIL 1493:

In his famous *Historia de las Indias*, contemporary Spanish historian Padre Bartolomé de las Casas described in full detail the glorious reception given Columbus by the Sovereigns at Barcelona. Since it is one of the very few authorities we have for that event, we will quote las Casas in full. Las Casas states:

> "He [Columbus] made the most haste he possibly could to reach Barcelona where he arrived the middle of April, and the Sovereigns were extremely solicitous to see him: and, having learned of his arrival, they ordered that a solemn and very beautiful reception should be given him, for which all the people came out and the whole city, filling the streets and marvelling on seeing in that venerable person the one who was said to have discovered another world, and on seeing the Indians and the parrots and the many nuggets and jewels and things made of gold which he had discovered and was carrying, and which never had been heard of or seen.[57]

> "For his reception the Sovereigns, with more solemnity and pomp, ordered their estrade and Royal throne placed in public where they were seated and with them the Prince Don Juan, very joyful in appearance and accompanied by many great Lords, Castilians, Catalonians, Valencians and Aragonese, all breathless and anxious for the arrival of the man who had accomplished such a great and heroic feat, and one which was a cause for rejoicing to all

---

57  Thacher, John Boyd, CHRISTOPHER COLUMBUS - HIS LIFE, HIS WORK, HIS REMAINS, VOLUME III, New York, 1904 [Public Domain], page 668. Underline and bold emphasis added by author.

Christianity. Then he entered the room where the Sovereigns were, accompanied by a multitude of noblemen and people of the highest rank, among all of whom, as he was tall and of commanding presence and looked like a Senator of the Roman people, his venerable countenance was distinguished crowned with grey hairs and with a modest smile showing plainly the joy and glory with which he came. Having first made them a profound acknowledgment, according to what was due to such great Princes, they arose to meet him as though he were one of the great Lords, and then drawing nearer, he knelt and begged them to give him their hands: they yielded to his entreaty with some reluctance and he having kissed their hands, they with most joyful faces ordered him to arise, and what was the supreme honour and favour among those which their Highnesses were accustomed to grant to very few Grandees, they ordered a stool [silla vasa] brought and that he should be seated in their Royal presence. He related very quietly and modestly the favours which God, in the venture of such Catholic Sovereigns, had shown him on his voyage, gave a particular account, as far as the time and season admitted of his route and discovery, and enumerated the greatness and felicity of the countries he had discovered, affirming the many more to be discovered, especially as at that time he thought the Island of Cuba was the main-land, according to what will be related farther on. <u>He showed the things which he brought which had not been seen, bringing out the large specimens of gold in beaten pieces although not very polished, and many large and small grains for smelting as they were taken from the earth, which he also carried;58</u> and he certified to the infinite amount which there was shown to be in those lands, and the confidence which must be reposed in their royal treasures as if the Sovereigns already had them gathered under their keys: and likewise what was the most precious treasure and to be thought most of, he told of the multitude and simplicity, meekness and nudity and customs of the people of these countries, and the very apt disposition and ability which he recognised in them to be brought to our Holy and Catholic faith: and there were present the Indians he took with him. Having heard all this and pondered upon it profoundly, the Catholic and most devout Princes arose and knelt down upon the floor and having joined their hands and raised them to Heaven, and with their eyes filled with tears, they commenced to give thanks to the Creator from the depths of their hearts: and as <u>the singers of the Royal chapel were there, in readiness and prepared, they sang *Te Deum Laudamus* and the high minstrels responded, so that it appeared that in that hour the celestial delights were opened and manifested to them and they communicated with them. Who can describe the tears which sprang from the Royal eyes and from the eyes of many Grandees of those realms who were there, and of all the persons of the Royal House? What joy, what pleasure, what ecstacy bathed the hearts of all!59</u> How some commenced to animate others and to propose in their hearts to come and settle these countries and aid in converting these people! Because they heard and saw that the most serene Princes and particularly the holy Queen Doña Isabella, by words and by the examples of their heroic works, gave all to understand that the principal pleasure and rejoicing of their souls proceeded from their having been found worthy before the Divine Presence; so that through their favour and by the expenditures [although very small] of their Royal Treasury, there should have been discovered

---

58   Ibid. Underline and bold emphasis added by author.
59   Underline and bold emphasis added by author.

so many unbelieving nations and so disposed, that in their times they might recognise their Creator and be reduced to the pale of His Holy and Universal Church, and His Catholic faith and Christian religion would be so immensely expanded.

"This immense and new joy was increased beyond comparison because our Lord ordered that it should come just at a time when the Catholic King, Don Ferdinand, was entirely recovered from a cruel knife-thrust which an unfortunate madman had given him in the neck, and which if he had not had on a golden collar like those which were worn then, would have wholly severed his throat. The demon inspired this man with the idea that if he killed him, he would be King. His Highness lay at the point of death from this wound, and as he was recently restored to health, inestimable festivities and rejoicings took place throughout all the Kingdom.

"So that Divine Providence ordained, in order to give to the Sovereigns and all the realms inestimable reason for rejoicing, that two such notable and joyful and new causes should occur together, which should spread among all kinds of persons such an abundance of spiritual and temporal happiness.

"Finally the Most Serene Sovereigns gave permission to the Admiral for that day that he should go to rest at the inn, to which he went, honourably accompanied by all the Court, by command of the Sovereigns.

"<u>During all the time that the Admiral remained in Barcelona, the Sovereigns increased his honours and favours each day.</u>[60] It was said that when the King rode through the city on horseback, he ordered the Admiral to go on one side of his Highness and the Infante on the other side, a favour which was for the Royal blood and which was not permitted to any other Grandee.

"Recognising these privileges, honours and favours which the Sovereigns bestowed upon the Admiral, as upon a person who had gained so much for them and merited so much, all the Grandees honoured and venerated him and were pleased only in doing so. They invited him to eat with them, each one when he was able to have him, some in order to serve the Sovereigns whom they beheld honouring and loving him so much, some because they saw that all had an interest in the service which he had rendered to the Sovereigns and the benefit which he was to all Spain, some from a desire to learn particularly of the great and wonderful countries and peoples and riches which he had discovered and the marvels which befell him, going and coming on his voyage."

---

60   Underline and bold emphasis added by author.

# KING FERDINAND PRESENTS SUIT OF ARMOR TO COLUMBUS

In Barcelona during the same period of time that Columbus received his new coat of arms, Markham reports another military gift:

> "Ferdinand also presented the Admiral with a splendid suit of Milanese armour, which is still preserved at the royal armory at Madrid."[61]

The Columbus suit of armor that Markham is referring to is undoubtedly the suit shown below in a circa 1880 print published by non-other than the Real Armeria itself:

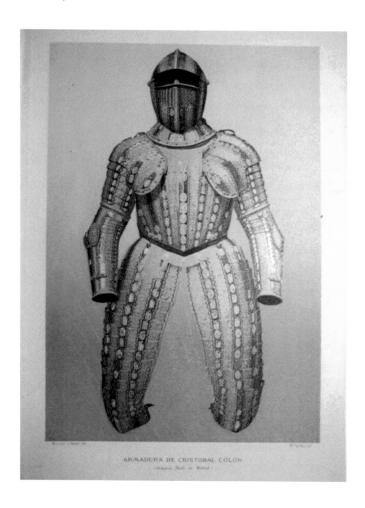

ARMADURA DE CRISTOBAL COLÓN

Armadura De Cristobal Colon (Armor of Christopher Columbus) is resplendent with silver and gold leaf details. When the lithograph is held up to the light, it is magnificent with bright metallic touches all over the suit of armor. This is an outstanding example of 19th century color lithography from LaFuente's Arte Espanol, published Madrid, circa 1880.

---

61   Markham, Clements R. (Clements Robert). Sir. 1830-1916. Life of Christopher Columbus. Philip & Son, London, January 1, 1892, page 139.

Unfortunately, this particular suit of armor was NEVER PRESENTED TO OR OWNED BY COLUMBUS. Any decent student of Medieval and/or Renaissance armor would tell you that this suit dates to 50 to maybe 100 years after Columbus' death. How such a revered institution as the Real Armeria could make such a mistake is actually easy to understand. During the Napoleonic Wars of the early 19th century, the Armeria was sacked at least twice. First, as the French troops approached Madrid, the citizens of Madrid raided it to get arms to defend the city. Next, after the victorious French occupied it, they to ravaged it to get some war trophies for themselves to take home. Undoubtedly, there most likely was a suit of Columbus's armor on their inventory list and when the curators could not find it, they simply put the tag on another suit that looked important. Whatever happened to Columbus' real suit of armor will likely never be known. It could still be in the basement of the Real Armeria, or a castle in France. We will never know because it has lost its provenance.

The importance of recounting this story here is simply to confirm the scope of lavish gifts Columbus received during the "honeymoon" period following the return from his First Voyage. The Queen even sent Columbus "bed-covers embroidered with the Admiral's arms—a gift at once regal and womanly."[62]

## LUXURIOUS ARMS & ARMOR WERE READILY AVAILABLE AND WERE EVEN MADE IN THE FIELD

As Washington Irving explains, luxurious arms and armor readily available – and were even made in the field. He uses the Siege of Baza in 1488 as an example:

"Thus, through the wonderful activity, judgment, and enterprise of this heroic and magnanimous woman [Queen Isabella], a great host, encamped in the heart of a warlike country, accessible only over mountain roads, was maintained in continual abundance. Nor was it supplied merely with the necessaries and comforts of life. The powerful escorts drew merchants and artificers from all parts, to repair, as if in caravans, to this great military market. In a little while, the camp abounded with tradesmen and artists of all kinds, to administer to the luxury and ostentation of the youthful chivalry. Here might be seen cunning artificers in steel, and accomplished armorers, achieving those rare and sumptuous helmets and cuirasses, richly gilt, inlaid, and embossed, in which the Spanish cavaliers delighted. Saddlers and harness-makers and horse milliners, also, were there, whose tents glittered with gorgeous

---

62    ANDRÉ DE HEVESY, THE DISCOVERER A NEW NARRATIVE OF THE LIFE AND HAZARDOUS ADVENTURES OF THE GENOESE
CHRISTOPHER COLUMBUS, New York 1928, page 186: "In this precarious situation, a ship arrived with a gift which cheered him mightily. It was a contribution from the Queen, toward the outfitting of the vice royal mansion, in the colony. There were one hundred hens and six roosters, seventy five pounds of fine soap, ten reams of writing paper, a supply of rose water and orange essence for his hands, a carpet, several tapestry hangings embroidered with trees and flowers, two chests of wood, a bed with two pillows made of fine cloth, six sheets of Holland weave, and bed-covers embroidered with the Admiral's arms—a gift at once regal and womanly."

housings and caparisons. The merchants spread forth their sumptuous silks, cloths, brocades, fine linen and tapestry."[63]

## COLUMBUS' GUN — GENERAL DESCRIPTION & OVERVIEW

- Spanish 15th Century Swivel-mounted Matchlock Espingole.
- Columbus' Name is Inscribed on the Barrel as part of His New 1493 Heraldic Motto.
- Profusely Adorned with Spanish Heraldic Reliefs made of New World Gold & Silver.
- Silver Coat of Arms of Ferdinand & Isabella as of 1492.
- Unique Da Vinci Lock: Pan Cover Rises Automatically As Serpentine Falls.
- Measures 50" In Length & Weighs Over 50 Lbs.

## THE COLUMBUS ESPINGOLE: THE KEY FEATURES POINTING TO CHRISTOPHER COLUMBUS AS THE RECIPIENT OF THE GUN:

## I. COLUMBUS' NAME IS INLAID IN THE BARREL IN THE FORM OF HIS 1493 PERSONAL MOTTO:

Barrel of Gun is Inscribed with the Heraldic Motto of Christopher Columbus, given to him by Ferdinand & Isabella on April 20, 1493 along with his new coat of arms after his return from the 1st Voyage. It was "POR CASTILLA Y POR LEON NUEVO MUNDO HALLO COLON" (Translation:

---

63   Washington Irving, A CHRONICLE OF THE CONQUEST OF GRANADA, New York, 1829, Vol. III, Co-operative Publishing Society Edition, pages 333 – 334, as sourced by Irving from Hernando del Pulgar, the historian and secretary to Queen Isabella, and who was also present at the siege of Baza. Pulgar recounted his experiences in his Chronicle of the Catholic Sovereigns.

For Castile and Leon Columbus has found the New World.) <u>This motto was only in use for a very short period of time, from 1493 – 1506.</u> After his death in 1506 several words in it were changed so as to read more in the past tense: "A CASTILLA Y A LEON NUEVO MUNDO DIO COLON." "Dio" meaning "gave," more in the past tense. It is the latter version that appears on Columbus's tomb at Seville, by order of King Ferdinand.[64]

64 JUSTIN WINSOR, <u>CHRISTOPHER COLUMBUS AND HOW HE RECEIVED AND IMPARTED THE SPIRIT OF DISCOVERY</u>, BOSTON AND NEW YORK, HOUGHTON, MIFFLIN AND COMPANY, The Riverside Press, Cambridge, 1891, [The Project Gutenberg Ebook # 42059 of Christopher Columbus and How He Received and Imparted the Spirit of Discovery by Justin Winsor], Page 258.

## II. DOCUMENTATION OF ESPINGOLE USE: FURNISHING ESPINGOLES IN MAY 1493 FOR COLUMBUS' SECOND VOYAGE:

— The Alcaide of Malaga ordered to furnish fifty "espingardas."

— The arsenal at the Alhambra ordered to furnish another fifty.

— Thus, a total of at least 100 Espingoles were on Second Voyage.

As De Navarrete documents:

From Malaga –

"NUMBER XXX. -- *Document for the Warden of Malaga to dispose* [i.e. dispatch] *for the armada of fifty breastplates and as many other espingarderos and crossbows.* (Registered in the Archive of the Indies in Sevilla.)"

"The King and the Queen: Garcia Fernandez Manrique, of our Council and our Warden in the city of Malaga: We have resolved to build a certain armada for the Island and Firm Land that are to be discovered and have been discovered in the Ocean in that part of the Indies, and that it would be armed and readied we have put at the head the Admiral Don Christopher Columbus and Don Juan of Fonseca, Archdeacon of Sevilla, of our Council: and thus it is necessary to send in said armada certain armaments, thus We order you that the armaments you should have there in the city of Malaga, that you should give them to the person written to you by the Admiral Don Christopher Columbus, and Don Juan of Fonseca, and Juan of Soria, Secretary of our Prince, our very esteemed and very beloved son, Deputy of our chief Accountants in the Treasury of said armada, fifty pairs of breastplates, and fifty espingarderos, and fifty crossbows; and take also all knowledge of said armaments that he were to give and hand over to you, with which and by our letter we do command that you be credited with said armaments. Dated in Barcelona on this twenty-third day of May of the year ninety-three."[65]

From the Alhambra –

"*Another letter was given to the Count of Tendilla, that of the armaments that are in the Alhambra, he would give fifty pairs of breastplates, and fifty* espingarderos, *and fifty crossbows. Dated in Barcelona on this twenty-third day of May of the year ninety-three.*"[66]

---

65  Don Martinez Fernandez De Navarrete, COLLECTION OF THE VOYAGES AND DISCOVERIES MADE BY THE SPANISH AT SEA SINCE THE END OF THE XV CENTURY, VOLUME II, SECOND EDITION, DOCUMENTS OF COLUMBUS AND OF THE FIRST POPULATIONS. By Order Of S.M. Madrid, Of The National Publishing House, 1859, page 54. This first-ever translation from Spanish to English was commissioned by the author.
66  Ibid.

<u>And to make sure there were enough trained Espingardero infantry to use them -</u>

*A Messenger document from the King and Queen dated September 1493 reads:*

"NUMBER LXXII. *Instructions that the.* may you be very well informed and from this here city, all things that were needed by you will be sent you.

Firstly, ten and six on horse, and two-hundred and fifty shield bearers and spearmen, and one-hundred and ten espingarderos (musketeers), and twenty Officers. (Legalized testimony in the Archive of the Indies in Sevilla, Leg. 5. of Royal Decree.)"[67]

## TREATMENT OF THE INDIANS –

Although it is not relevant to the theme of this book, the author cannot ignore that the same pages of this Royal Decree also instruct Columbus on how he should treat the Taino Indians:

"The main task you are to do is to safe guard the Indians, that no harm be done to them, nor that anything be taken from them against their will, but that they would receive honor, and that they would be safeguarded so as to be upset in no way."[68]

"... that there may be no cause of any person of any rank or condition at all, that may take anything from the Indians and cause two-thousand angers: and this would be something very against the will of and in disservice to the King and the Queen, for their Highnesses desire more the Salvation of these people that they might be Christians, than all the riches that can come out of it, so let it be known...."[69]

## III. LOCK DECORATION CONTAINS BUST OF COLUMBUS:

The lockplate, the central focus of the gun, sports a Silver Bas-Relief Bust said to be that of Columbus. Note that his ruddy cheeks, aquiline nose is similar to other known drawings and paintings of him, and this bust also fits the physical description of Columbus made by his son Bartholomew. Also note that he is wearing a distinctly 1490's Archer's Salad (not a mid-1500's style of Morion or Cabasset helmet). See photo below of an example from the Harold Peterson Collection.[70]

---

67  Ibid., page 125 - 126.
68  Ibid.
69  Ibid., page 127.
70  Harold L. Peterson, <u>Arms and Armor in Colonial America 1526 - 1783</u>, New York, 1956, page 109.

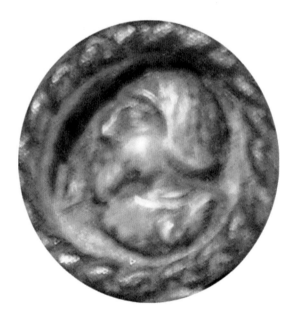

*Author's Collection and Joe Kindig, Jr. Collection*
Plate 117. Italian archer's salades, late 15th century and early 16th century, indicating the evolution of the type.

## IV. 1496 DRAWING OF COLUMBUS-STYLE ESPINGOLES AT COLUMBUS' SANTO DOMINGO FORT:

**A 16th century plan of the defenses of Santo Domingo, the oldest city in the New World. Ships appear in the harbor at the right.**[71]

71  McKendrick, Melveena, Ferdinand and Isabella, New York, 1968, Page 84, crediting Bradley Smith, Spain: A History in Art. Simon & Schuster, New York, 1966.

# THE COLUMBUS ESPINGOLE: THE KEY FEATURES POINTING TO QUEEN ISABELLA AS THE PRESENTER OF THE GUN

## A. 1492 COAT OF ARMS OF FERDINAND & ISABELLA WITH THE POMEGRANATE

The Silver Appliquéd Coat of Arms of Ferdinand & Isabella with the Pomegranate, heraldic symbol of Grenada (which was only used on their coat of arms from after the conquest of Granada in 1492 until 1504, when Isabella died).

## B. QUEEN ISABELLA'S HERALDIC RELIEFS

Gun is Profusely Adorned with Isabella's Heraldic Reliefs made of silver and New World Gold: The Lion Rampant (symbolizing the Kingdom of Leon); and the Castle (symbolizing the Kingdom of Castille) . <u>There are no heraldic reliefs representing King Ferdinand (the bars and eagle) on the gun because Ferdinand's kingdoms of Aragon and Sicily did not contribute to the funding of Columbus' voyages – only Isabella's did.</u> In the decades to come only Isabella's subjects, Castillians, were even allowed to go to the Nuevo Mundo (the New World), but not Ferdinand's. This distinction was immortalized in the famous old Hollywood movie: *The Captain from Castille.*

**EAGLE OF SAINT JOHN: another Silver Appliquéd symbol associated with the Catholic Kings, namely the Eagle of Saint John, is all over the stock & barrel. It was replaced after death of Ferdinand & Isabella by the Double-Headed Papal, or Hapsburg, Eagle.**

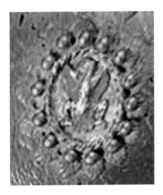 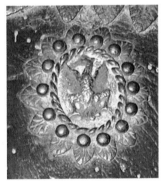  

The better known heraldic use of the Eagle of St. John has been the single supporter chosen by Queen Isabella of Castile in her armorial achievement used as heiress and later integrated into the heraldry of the Catholic Monarchs. This election alludes to the queen's great devotion to the evangelist that predated her accession to the throne.[72]

---

72   VV. AA., *Isabel la Católica en la Real Academia de la Historia*, Real Academia de la Historia, 2004. <u>ISBN</u> <u>978-84-95983-54-1</u>. Cfr. para la heráldica de Isabel y Fernando las <u>pp. 72 & ff.</u>

The Eagle of St. John was placed on side of the shields used as English consort by Catherine of Aragon, daughter of the Catholic Monarchs, Mary I and King Philip as English monarchs.

Did Da Vinci ever meet Queen Isabella and/or Columbus? After all, they were contemporaries. The discovery of the dairy and letters of Beatrix Galinda (Latin tutor to Queen Isabella at University of Salamanca) describe their meeting and relationship, as will be discussed later.[73]

---

73   Abeniam, Jacques, <u>DA VINCI SFUMATO – The Revelation </u>by, ISBN 978-0-9812591-1-6, pages 3-6.

# LOCK, STOCK & BARREL – THE COLUMBUS ESPINGOLE EXAMINED

## SIMILAR FEATURES ON OTHER EARLY STYLE ARQUEBUSES

Recall that the arquebuses pictured above in the Codex Monacensis 222, circa 1500 and other early Codices show stark similarities to the Columbus Espingole:

a)  Serpentine match holder;

b)  Muzzle Shape;

c)  Barrel Shape;

d)  Stock Shape;

e)  Rear Sight; and

f)  Ramrod.

## 1. THE LOCK

The lost Madrid Codices of Leonardo da Vinci show his matchlock design, circa 1491, with an Automatic – Opening Pan Cover. The design of Leonardo's mechanism and its operation are not just similar to the Columbus gun….they are exactly the same.

Prior to the discovery of these lost CODEX manuscripts, a few scholars had questioned that such a never-before-seen advanced lock mechanism on the Columbus gun as being an (academically un-welcome) "anomaly." Obviously, this discovery clearly documents that the automatic-opening pan cover on the "Columbus" matchlock is not an anomaly after all, as the lost Codices of Leonardo da Vinci pictures the exact device circa 1490-1491.

The lock is of wonderfully wrought of iron or steel. The serpentine match holder is the head of an intricately wrought iron dragon. The lock has another unique feature that has not been seen before: as the giant tiller-trigger is pulled, there is a wrought iron flash pan cover that lifts up simultaneously to expose the priming powder to the match!

On the lock plate are two small silver plaques: a lion rampant and a profile head of a bearded man thought to be Christopher Columbus. There is also a solid gold lion's head full-face.

# THE LOCK

**Note the flashpan is a "Horn of Plenty" symbolizing the riches of the New World.**

# LOCK DECORATIONS:

**Bust of Columbus ?**
**1490's archer's Salet, not cabasset/morion**
**Gold Lion's Head**
**LION OF LEON**

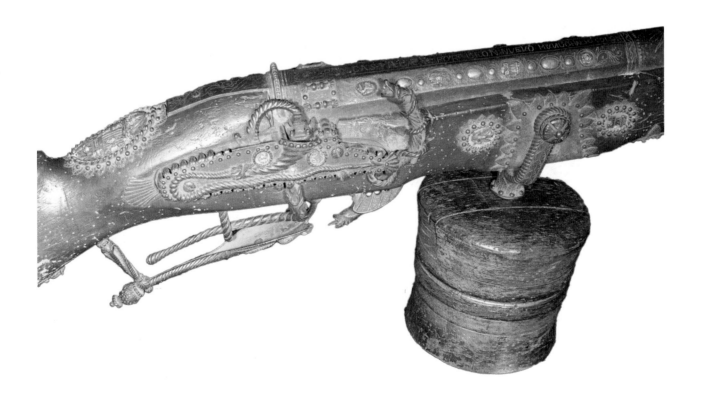

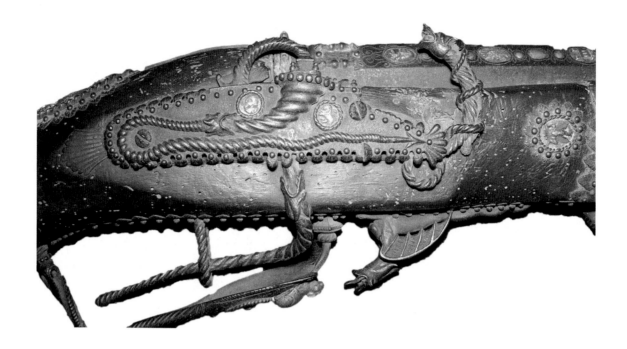

**Below: A look at the flashpan cover being raised enough to reveal the touchhole.**

A close-up view of the intricate workmanship of the serpentine
Dragon's Head Match Holder.

View of the lock's back plate.

## JUST HOW UNIQUE IS LEONARDO'S LOCK MECHANISM COMPARED TO OTHER MATCHLOCKS?

Just how unique is Leonardo's lock mechanism compared to other contemporary matchlocks?

Probably the most comprehensive study on matchlock mechanisms and cited by Harold L. Peterson[74] is Thierbach Moritz's <u>Die Geschichtliche Entwickelung der Handfeuerwaffen.</u>[75]

Plates 1, 2 and 3 illustrated below show well over 50 distinct matchlock ignition mechanisms. Not a single one of them remotely resembles Da Vinci's Automatic-Opening Flashpan Cover mechanism.

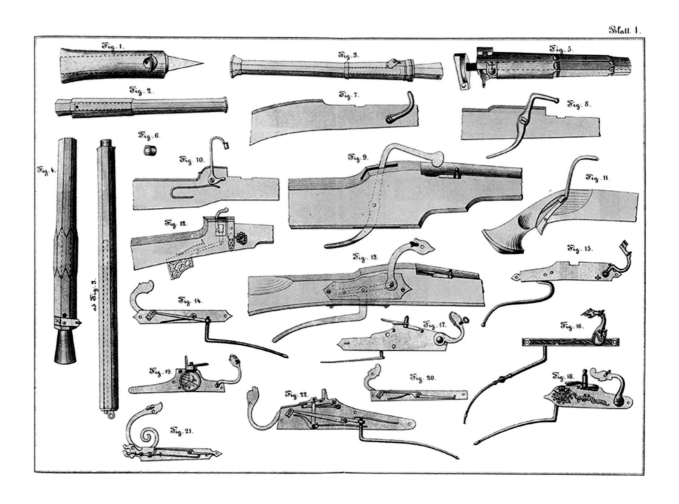

---

74    Harold L. Peterson, Arms and Armor in Colonial America, 1526-1783., New York, 1956, page 50.
75    Thierbach Moritz, <u>Die Geschichtliche Entwickelung der Handfeuerwaffen Bearb. Nach den Deutschen Sammlungen Noch Vorhandenen Originalen.</u> Dresden 1888. See Pates 1, 2 and 3.

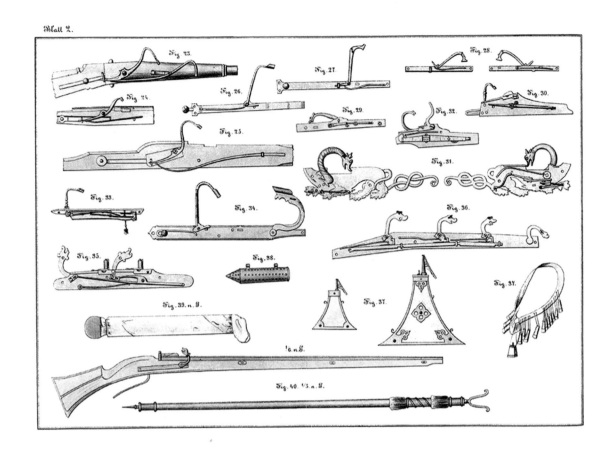

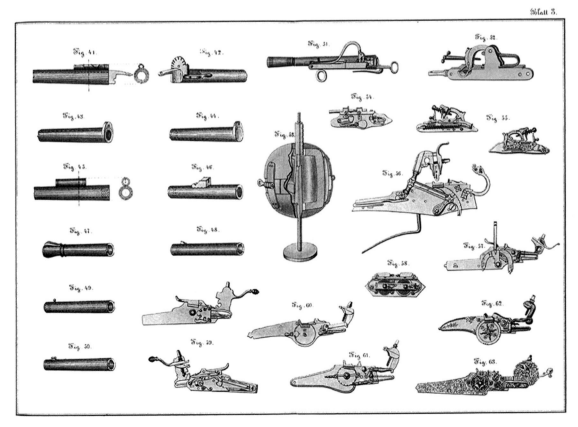

Forward-Sliding Automatic-Opening Pan Covers on German Matchlocks, ca. 1560-1650

At this point the author wishes to take note of the existance of 1510 – 1570's Post-Leonardo/Columbus Gun Automatic-Opening Pan Covers, even though they are of a very different mechanical nature. See Figures 17, 19 and 22 in Thierbach's Plate 1 above.

This feature is extremely rare to find on German military matchlock muskets, and all those pieces [reported in the internet blog cited here] are equipped with a matchlock mechanism, but a lock plate which has the shape of a wheel-lock.[76]

The automatically-opening pan cover has been adopted from the earlier 1510 – 1520s wheel-lock; in some cases it even appears on matchlock mechanisms which actually are pretending to be wheel-locks and are only identifiable as matchlocks upon a second and closer look.

One of the earliest known examples is in internet blogger Michael's very impressive collection. It is the first illustrated in his blog, clearly pretending to be a wheel-lock and made in ca. 1560, most probably in Augsburg. It's actually a snap matchlock. The pan cover has to be shut manually, then the serpentine with a length of match cord is cocked and when the trigger is pulled it snaps down into the pan, simultaneously pushing open the sliding cover. Even the safety catch is the same as on wheel-locks.

Thus, there were three Types of Post-Leonardo/Columbus Gun Automatic-Opening Pan Covers:

I – Wheellock 1510 – 25 – A toggle-actuated automatic-opening pan cover. When released, the wheel activates a small toggle which flips the swivel-mounted flat pan cover open to the right (Fig. 2 - Palazzo Ducale, Venice example).

II – Wheellock 1520's on - A more sturdy design in which the pan cover is pushed forward in line with the barrel by an inner-lock lever which uncovers the flash pan (Figure 4 - Landeszeughaus, Graz example).

III – Matchlock 1540 – 70 - A Snap Matchlock mechanism in which the pan cover is pushed forward by an inner-lock lever set in motion by the falling Serpentine (the German example from "Michael's" blog edited by "Matchlock").[77]

---

76   *From "Michael's" blog on VikingSwords.com Last edited by Matchlock : 8th August 2010 at 06:15 PM.* Matchlock - Member. Join Date: Sep 2008. Location: Bavaria, Germany, the center of 15th and 16th century gun making.
77   Ibid.

## 2. THE STOCK

The stock of the Columbus Espingole pictured above shows stark similarities to the arquebuses in the Codex Monacensis 222, circa 1500, and in other early Codices illustrated and discussed above.

Also, other similar early style arquebuses are pictured in many of the Rodrigio Aleman wood carvings, dating 1492 – 1494 in the Toledo Cathedral, including the BOMBARDMENT of GRENADA – 1492:[78]

> "The lower rank of the choir stalls of Toledo cathedral contains masterpieces of late medieval art, carved between 1489 and 1495 by Rodrigo Aleman, a German craftsman who made his way to Spain in the late fifteenth century. Surviving documents tell us a great deal about him and indicate his influence on Iberian wood carving at the dawn of the Renaissance. The choir stalls of Toledo cathedral are among his earliest recorded commissions, and he may have risen to prominence through these works.
>
> The outstanding features of these stalls are the carved panels set into the back of each seat and into the railings which connect them. In all, Master Rodrigo carved 54 panels, each enlivened

---

78    James D. Ryan, THE CHOIR STALLS OF TOLEDO AND THE CRUSADE TO CAPTURE GRENADA, New York, 2004. See also: Juan de Mata Carriazo, LOS RELIEVES DE LA GUERRA DE GRANADA EN LA SILLERIA DEL CORE DE LA CATEDRAL DE TOLEDO, Madrid, 1985.

with a scene from the war in Granada, a nine-year struggle still in progress when Rodrigo began his work. His craftsmanship was praised at the time as a faithful representation of the final campaigns of the Reconquista. That was surely the plan of Master Rodrigo's employer, Cardinal Mendoza, who was himself a participant in the war in Granada. Archeological considerations aside, the 54 panels are exquisite examples of the carver's art. Each is 56 cm. wide and 37 cm. high (21 inches by 14 inches), sculpted in bas-relief from a single plank of Spanish walnut."

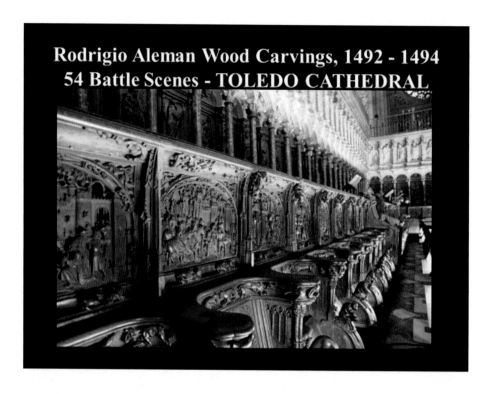

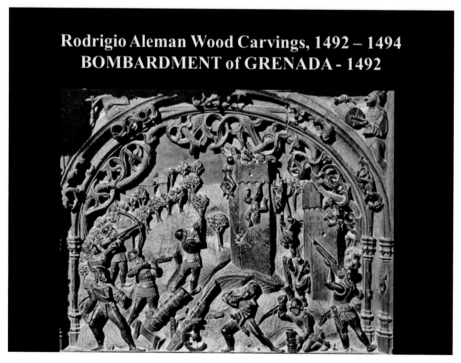

On the right side of the stock near the swivel are silver plaques: a castle and the eagle displayed. The cherry wood stock also points to Spanish manufacture.

Forward of the trigger guard is a beautifully wrought, large, winged dragon with solid gold eyes. The guard is decorated with three of the gold lion's heads, a large silver crouched rabbit cast and chased in the round, and a large, silver, high-relief, full-face head of Pan. Forward of the swivel on the underside of the stock is another large, high-relief silver plaque: a profiled Moor's head of Negroid type with curly hair.

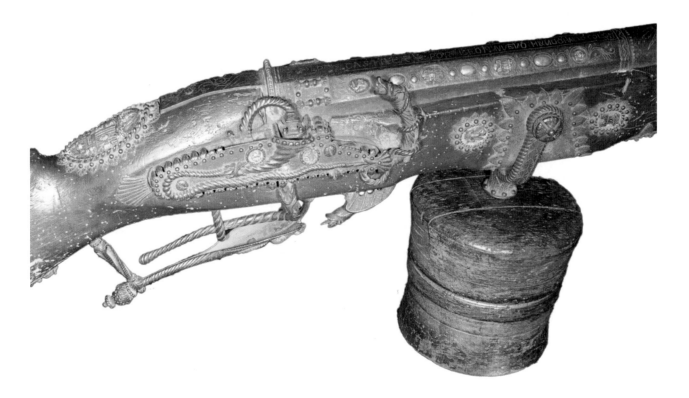

**Evidence of a lot of hard use in the New World:** Note the slight bending of the yoke that undoubtedly came from the stress of repeated firing from a ship's rail or other fixed position. Later, but probably during its period of use, the yoke was horizontally rotated to even out the stress on it.

# 3. THE BARREL

The barrel of the Columbus Espingole pictured above shows stark similarities to the arquebuses in the Codex Monacensis 222, circa 1500, and other early Codices illustrated and discussed above.

The rear end of the barrel is of octagonal cross-section. It and the barrel tang are very richly decorated, being inlaid, or incised, with silver filigree in the same hand as the similar décor on the barrel. The rear right is of brass.

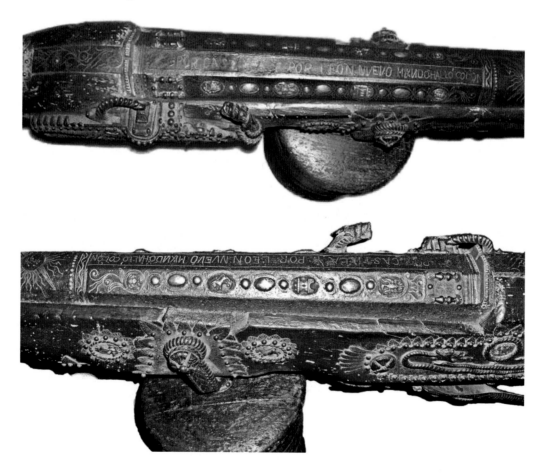

The front sight is of wrought steel:

The muzzle and front end of the barrel is round and the tip is ornamented with a twisted iron band of "rope" design. It is also decorated with a band of pomegranate-shaped studs with beads imitating pomegranate seeds. On the top of the barrel a crescent moon and the sun are damascened in silver by the same hand as all of the other incised barrel decor.

**It is said that the beading decoration on almost every part of the gun are considered characteristic of the Pamplona (Navarra) region of Spain.**

# THE HERALDIC FEATURES ON
# THE COLUMBUS GUN

## HERALDRY & ROYAL COATS OF ARMS AS A METHOD OF DATING ARTIFACTS

## HERALDRY & ROYAL COATS OF ARMS AS A METHOD OF DATING ARTIFACTS

HERALDRY was an important aspect of chivalry in the Middle Ages, and a system for identifying European aristocracy as well.

In the case of royalty, it was also a means
for showing the territories
governed by a particular dynasty.

Royal Coats of Arms frequently changed,
not only from ruler-to-ruler,
but often from year-to-year within the reign of a monarch
to reflect a recent territorial conquest.

# THE ROYAL COAT OF ARMS OF THE CATHOLIC KINGS 1492 – 1506

## Royal Standard of the Catholic Kings 1492-1506

After the conquest of Granada a pomegranate was added to the base of the shield.

The symbols associated to the (first) Catholic Kings, namely the eagle of Saint John, the yoke and arrows and the motto *Tanto Monta, Monta Tanto*, as well as other traditional, pre-Catholic Kings' symbols such as the *royal bend* of Castile, gradually disappeared from Spanish coats-of-arms and flags along the 16th century, as Austrian and Burgundian symbols became gradually more frequent.

Thus, the eagle of Saint John —which is basically a black (sometimes *proper*) eagle displayed with wings inverted and a nimbus behind its head— was replaced with the Austrian double-headed eagle.

The *Tanto Monta, Monta Tanto* motto was substituted by the *Plus Ultra*.

The yoke and arrows were replaced with the pillars of Hercules, etc.

**Silver 1492 Coat of Arms of Ferdinand & Isabella on the wrist stock:**

La cronica de España.

Ferdinand and Isabella's coat of arms (above), from a 1493 Spanish *Historia*, stresses their equal majesty by quartering the castles and lions of her Castile and Leon with the bars and eagles of his Aragon and Sicily. The yoke and the arrows are the personal badges of King Ferdinand and Queen Isabella. Yoke (*yugo*) for Ysabel and arrows (*flechas*) for Ferdinand.[79]

---

79  McKendrick, Melveena, Ferdinand and Isabella, New York, 1968, Page 30, crediting Valera, La Cronica de Espana, 1493: Biblioteca Nacional, Madrid.

## COINS OF THE REALM - THE DOUBLOON - ALSO CONFIRM DATES

### Front side of coin

### Back side - Pre-1492 (no Pomegranate)

## Back side - 1492 – 1516 (with Pomegranate)

Treasures of Maryland

# AFTER FERDINAND & ISABELLA: CHARLES V (EVERYTHING CHANGES)

**The Coat of Arms of Charles V (1516 – 1556) displays all of the central European, Spanish and Mediterranean territories linked to his family:**
**Castile, Leon, Aragon, Sicily, Modern Austria, Ancient Burgundy, Modern Burgundy, Brabant, Flanders and the Tyrol.**
**His personal motto "PLVS VLTER" ("Further Beyond") encircled the Pillars of Hercules, all symbolizing the post-Columbus conquests of the new world and beyond.**
**(no Pomegranate)**
**His prominent display of the Order of the Golden Fleece also emphasized his Burgundian family ties.**

# THE HELMET OF CHARLES V – BURGUNDIAN DÉCOR WITH NO POMEGRANATES IN SIGHT

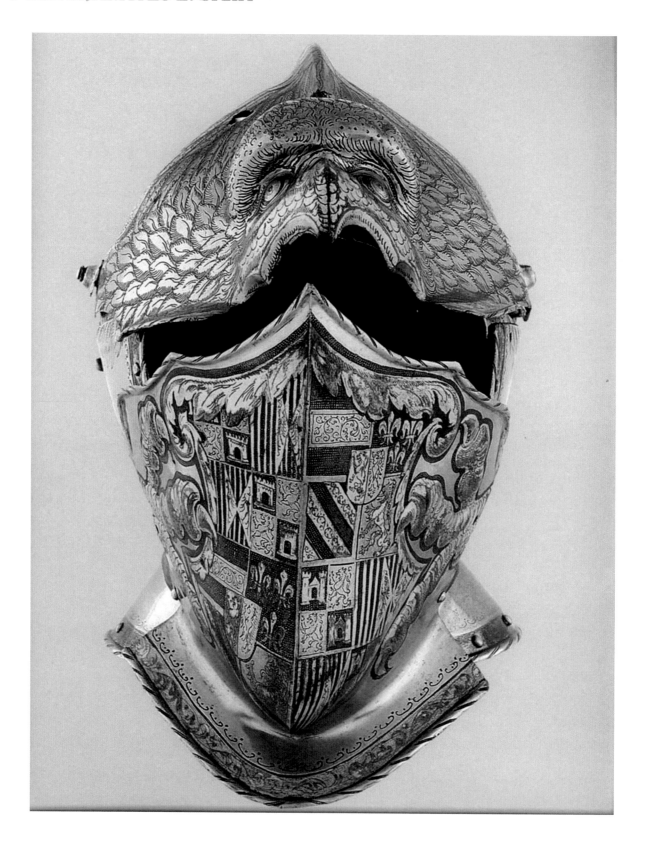

# THE SADDLE OF CHARLES V – NOTE THE APPEARANCE OF THE PILLARS OF HERCULES AND THE BURGUNDIAN DOUBLE-HEADED EAGLE (REPLACING THE EAGLE OF ST. JOHN)

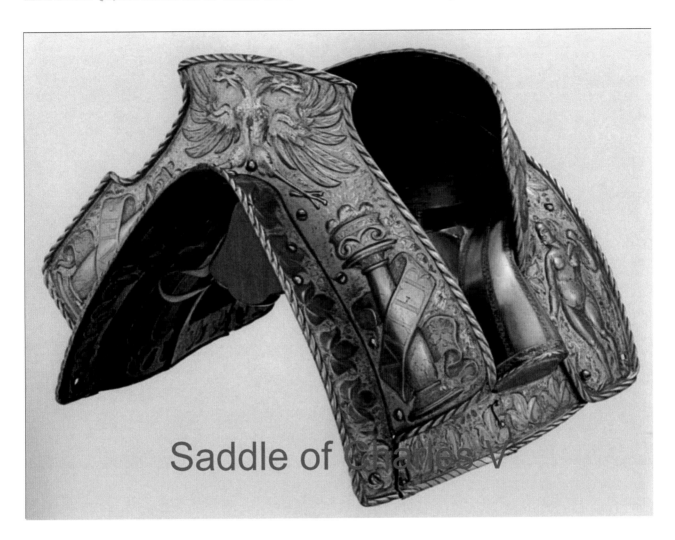

Saddle of Charles V

## THE HERALDIC MOTTO OF COLUMBUS ON THE BARREL

# THE HERALDIC MOTTO OF CHRISTOPHER COLUMBUS:

## POR CASTILLA Y POR LEON NUEVO MUNDO HALLO COLON

"For Castile and for Leon, Columbus has discovered a New World."

[First appearance of Columbus's new Motto was in April, 1493
on a white banner of the Admiral,
bearing the arms which had been granted to him by the Sovereigns
upon his glorious return from the New World and Entry into Barcelona]

[Last Appearance of Columbus's Motto: On his Tomb]
"A Castilla Y a Leon, Nuevo Mundo dió Colon"

Note Change from "HALLO" to "DIO"
"Has Discovered" vs. "Gave Us" [past tense]

Alongside the Motto are inlaid several pairs of raised silver plaques, matching on both sides of the barrel. These consist (each side) of three plain oval Egg plaques and six plain round Eggs, plus another four plaques cast in high relief as follows:

- a winged human head of Medusa

- a Lion rampant (the Kingdom of Leon)

- a Castle (the Kingdom of Castile)

- an Eagle displayed (the Eagle of St. John)

- nine oval and round Eggs

# For "CASTILLA" & "LEON" Why not "ARAGON" ?

**Because Aragon was King Ferdinand's kingdom and he did not sponsor Columbus' voyage, only Isabella (King of Castille and Leon) sponsored Columbus.**

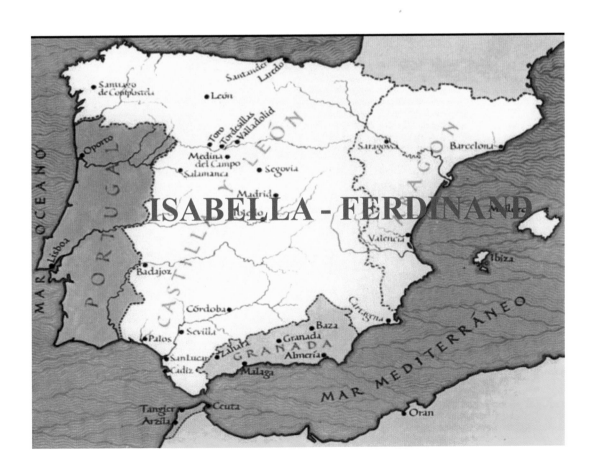

## COLUMBUS' NEW COAT OF ARMS AND MOTTO AS GIVEN TO HIM ON APRIL 20, 1493

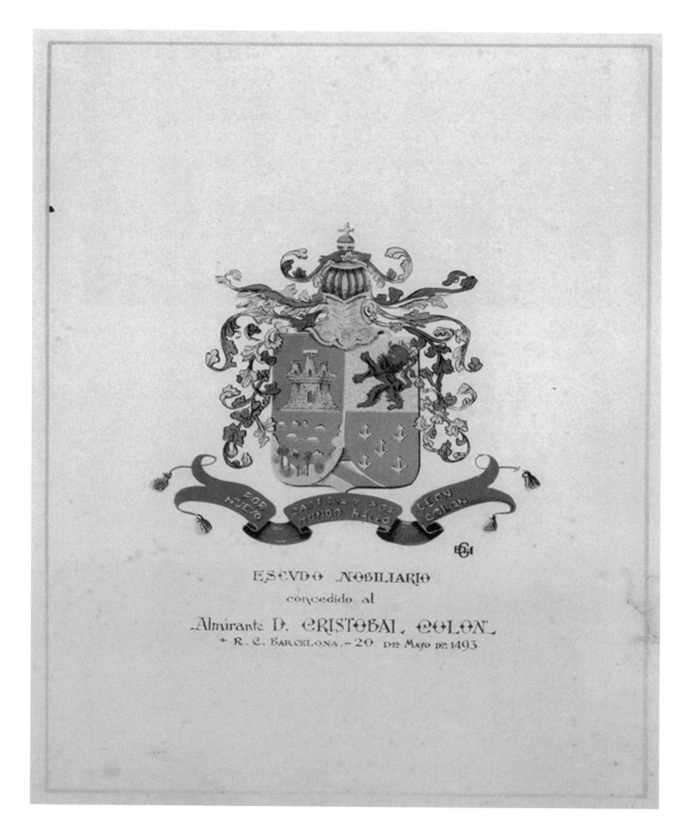

# THE LA RABIDA VARIATION OF COLUMBUS' NEW COAT OF ARMS

## QUEEN ISABELLA'S HERALDIC RELIEFS

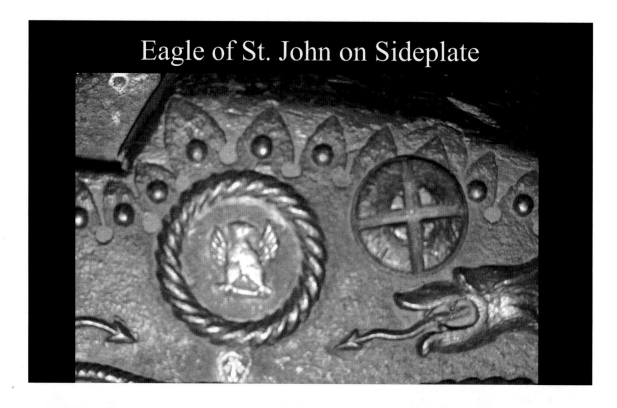

Eagle of St. John on Sideplate

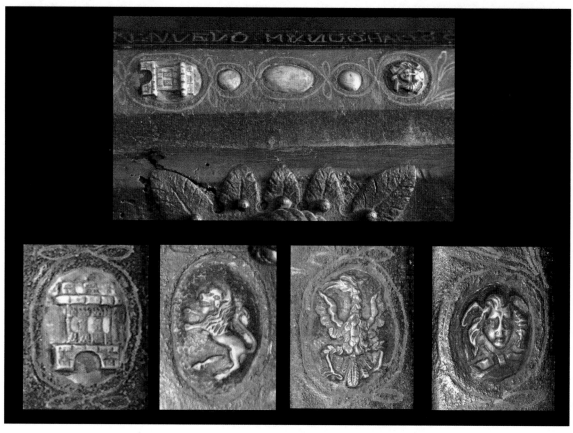

# THE IMPORTANCE OF THE POMEGRANATE CANNOT BE UNDERESTIMATED

The silver Pomegranate heraldic reliefs, the pomegranate leaf petaloid edge decoration and the tiny full-round pomegranate seeds all symbolize and celebrate the great Spanish Conquest of Granada in 1492.

ISABELLA'S CROWN – 1492
Note the Pomegranates

## POMEGRANATE LEAF PETALOID EDGE DECORATION – A UNIFYING THEME ON EVERY PART OF THE GUN: LOCK, STOCK & BARREL

There is a broad forend barrel band of wrought steel with petaloid decorations on the rear edge. This same petaloid edge decoration appears on the edges of the lock plate, as well as the side plate, trigger guard, barrel bands, decorative heraldic medallions, swivel yoke, and even the tip of the muzzle -- thus showing all parts of the gun to be congruent, original and contemporary with each other. This also goes to show that the gun was made and assembled all at one time, and not the amalgamation of an older arquebus with later-added decorations. All metal parts are decorated with the prolific beading considered characteristic of Pamplona (Navarra). The profuse use of fully round beads everywhere on every part of the gun (instead of the usual half-rounded tacks or nails) alongside the pomegranate leaf clearly indicates that these tiny balls represent the little round seeds of the pomegranate.

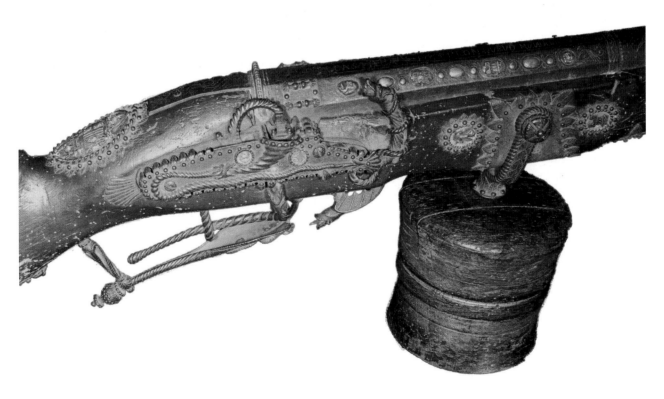

# THE MEANING OF THE ALLEGORICAL DECORATIVE SCULPTURE OF: THE RABBIT AGAINST THE DRAGON: SPAIN AGAINST THE SEA OF DARKNESS

At first glance this scene of a little silver rabbit facing off a fearsome dragon seems absolutely preposterous. The adorable rabbit looks like a one-bite appetizer. However, the rabbit and dragon turn out to allegorical players on the stage of history. While in Medieval times the hare, or rabbit, was also a symbol of fertility and of timidity, it is simply absurd to even think of a rabbit confronting a dragon unless both the dragon and the rabbit symbolized something else.[80]

The scene plays out on the trigger guard in the gold, silver & iron sculpture of this rabbit facing off (in an elevated position) against a dragon. As we shall soon see in this face-off, the rabbit is the allegorical symbol of Spain. "Espana" (Spain) in ancient Carthaginian and Latin meant "Land of the Rabbits."

The Dragon represents the Sea of Darkness on the Columbus gun and symbolizes Spain's struggle to conquer the Sea of Darkness (the Atlantic Ocean), which in Medieval times was often represented as being full of dragons and sea serpents ready to devour the unlucky ships which might venture too far west.

Dragons and sea monsters were often shown on medieval maps in the Atlantic Ocean, symbolizing it as an impenetrable and dangerous "Sea of Darkness." Note that the rabbit on the Columbus gun is in the superior, elevated, and "Winning" position relative to the dragon in this sculpture.

---

80    See: Simona Cohen, <u>ANIMALS AS DISGUISED SYMBOLS IN RENAISSANCE ART</u>, Netherlands, 2008.

# HOW DRAGONS CAME TO REPRESENT THE SEA OF DARKNESS:

How Dragons came to represent the Sea of Darkness was well-explained by H.E. Marshall:

"In those far-off times besides the Vikings of the North other daring sailors sailed the seas. But all their sailings took them eastward. For it was from the east that all the trade and the riches came in those days. To India and to far Cathay sailed the merchant through the Red Sea and the Indian Ocean, to return with a rich and fragrant cargo of silks and spices, pearls and priceless gems."

"None thought of sailing westward. For to men of those days the Atlantic Ocean was known as the Outer Sea or the Sea of Darkness. There was nothing to be gained by venturing upon it, much to be dreaded. It was said that huge and horrible sea-dragons lived there, ready to wreck and swallow down any vessel that might venture near. An enormous bird also hovered in the skies waiting to pounce upon vessels and bear them away to some unknown eyrie. Even if any foolhardy adventurers should defy these dangers, and escape the horror of the dragons and the bird, other perils threatened them. For far in the west there lay a bottomless pit of seething fire. That was easy of proof. Did not the face of the setting sun glow with the reflected light as it sank in the west? There would be no hope nor rescue for any ship that should be drawn into that awful pit."

"Again it was believed that the ocean flowed downhill, and that if a ship sailed down too far it would never be able to get back again. These and many other dangers, said [the ignorant people of those days, threatened the rash sailors who should attempt to sail upon the Sea of Darkness. So it was not wonderful that for hundreds of years men contented themselves with the well-known routes which indeed offered adventure enough to satisfy the heart of the most daring."

"But as time passed these old trade-routes fell more and more into the hands of Turks and Infidels. Port after port came under their rule, and infidel pirates swarmed in the Indian Ocean and Mediterranean until no Christian vessel was safe. At every step Christian traders found themselves hampered and hindered, and in danger of their lives, and they began to long for another way to the lands of spice and pearls."

"Then it was that men turned their thoughts to the dread Sea of Darkness. The less ignorant among them had begun to disbelieve the tales of dragons and fiery pits. The world was round, said wise men. Why then, if that were so, India could be reached by sailing west as well as by sailing east."

"Many men now came to this conclusion, among them an Italian sailor named Christopher Columbus. The more Columbus thought about his plan of sailing west to reach India, the more he believed in it, and the more he longed to set out. But without a great deal of money such an expedition was impossible, and Columbus was poor. His only hope was to win the help and friendship of a king or some other great and wealthy person."[81]

Prestigious map historian and Columbus scholar, Chet Van Duzer, has lectured about ancient maps and sea monsters at the Library of Congress, among many other institutions. He references Olaus Magnus's Carta marina of 1539 in his ground-breaking work: Sea Monsters on Medieval and Renaissance Maps.[82]

## The Sea of Darkness[83]

---

81    *Henrietta Elizabeth Marshall*, This Country of Ours – The Story of the United States, Chapter II - The Sea Of Darkness And The Great Faith Of Columbus, *New York, 1917, pages 14 - 15. This work has been selected by scholars over the years as being culturally important, and is part of the knowledge base of civilization as we know it.*

82    Chet van Duzer, Sea Monsters on Medieval and Renaissance Maps, British Library, 2014.

83    Magnus, Claus, "The Sea Of Darkness" Original caption: "The Sea of Darkness;" Woodcut of a sea snake by Olaus Magnus, 1555.

# A Sea Snake Monster

**Note: the sailor is defending the ship with a shoulder-fired Arquebus.[84]**

84    16th Woodcut from Zvi Dor-Ner, <u>COLUMBUS AND THE AGE OF DISCOVERY</u>, New York, 1991, page 23.

## HOW RABBITS CAME TO REPRESENT SPAIN:

The country's name has taken some interesting turns:

— It was first named Iberia from the word for river in 6000 BCE.

— This changed to Hesperia (Land of the setting sun) in 600 BCE by the Greeks.

— Then the Carthaginians changed it to Ispania ( Land of the rabbits) in 300 BCE.

— The Romans more or less kept the name as Hispania.

— From Medieval to modern times the Spanish called their country España, but now the meaning is pretty much lost in modern times.

**Views of the solid silver sculpture of a rabbit facing off against a dragon, allegorical symbolism of Spain (rabbit), conquering the "Sea of Darkness" – the unknown. Dragons & sea monsters were often shown on medieval maps in the Atlantic Ocean, symbolizing it as an impenetrable and dangerous "Sea of Darkness" – conquered by Columbus. Note the dragon's New World gold eyes & lion heads (Leon).**

## THE MOOR'S HEAD

The Silver Moor's Head on the Columbus gun is located on the bottom side of the stock between the swivel yoke and the entrance of the ramrod. Like all other parts of the gun, it is embellished with the pomegranate leaf edging and round pomegranate seeds. The Moor's Head was frequently used as a heraldic symbol in Medieval times for conquests in the Middle East and/or Africa.

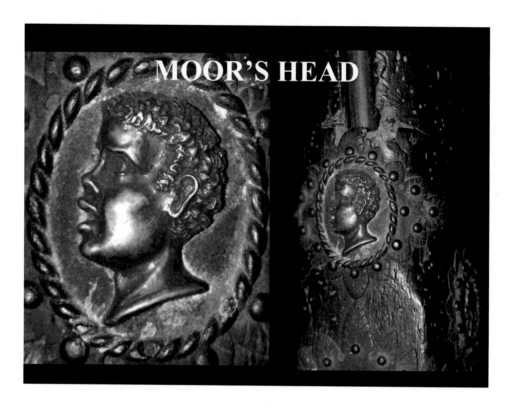

As pressure from the Reyes Católicos (the Christian Reconquistadors) increased over the centuries, African states in Spain mutated and fell and rose many times. The most stable and longest lived African state in Spain was Grenada, with the magnificent Nasridin dynasty citadel of Al Hambra as its capitol. Al Hambra surrendered to the Reyes Católicos at dawn on January 2, 1492. Spain and Portugal followed this action with the conquest of parts of Africa, the destruction of African communities in Europe and the invasion of the Americas. Lisbon's black population, that out-numbered Europeans in 1550, was devasted by the plagues of the times. The last free blacks in Spain were expelled on April 6, 1609.[85]

---

85   Internet Blog Posting: Ivan Sache, 18 Febuary 2001. Return to Moran Coats of Arms. Above taken from Victoria & Albert Museum: http://www.vam.ac.uk/collections/periods_styles/medieval/hidden_histories_africans/heraldry/index.html Even long before the Crusades, on April 30 in 711, at the invitation of the sons of the late Visigoth King Wittiza, the Umayyad General Tarikh ibn Ziyad (el Moro) led 7000 troops into what was to became Spain and Portugal. His troops consisted of 300 Arabs and 6,700 native Africans. Ibn Husayn (ca. 950) recorded that these troops were "Sudanese", the Arabic word for Black people. The banner of the Maure, the negro head blindfolded on a white background, became associated with Tarik's African armies.

<u>Conclusion</u>: Its meaning is clear. The Moor's Head symbolizes the Reconquest of Spain completed in 1492 by Ferdinand and Isabella's capture of Grenada, the last remaining Moorish stronghold in Spain.

# HEAD OF PAN ON COLUMBUS GUN

The head of Pan appears on the underside (trigger guard) of the Columbus gun.

Pan (Greek Πάν), in Greek religion and mythology, is the god of shepherds and flocks, of mountain wilds, hunting, and rustic music, as well as the companion of the nymphs.[86] His name originates within the Greek language, from the word *paein* (Πάειν), meaning "to pasture."[87] He has the hind-quarters, legs, and horns of a goat, in the same manner as a faun or satyr. With his homeland in rustic Arcadia, he is recognized as the god of fields, groves, and wooded glens; because of this, Pan is connected to fertility and the season of spring. Pan-Satyr stands for Fertility & Nature. To

---

86    From Wikipedia, the free encyclopedia. See also: "Pan" (Greek mythology) entry in Collins English Dictionary; and Edwin L. Brown, "The Lycidas of Theocritus Idyll 7", Harvard Studies in Classical Philology, 1981:59–100.

87    See: <u>Pan • Facts and Information on the God Pan</u>. See: greekgodsandgoddesses.net › gods › pan.

the Greeks, Pan was a shepherd: he was half goat and half man, a thing of nature certainly not the Antichrist or a being who was out to corrupt and steal men's souls. He was lusty; he played pipes and was therefore musical; and he was a god of nature.

## Faces of the Greek God Pan

Faces of Pan generally depict a man with horns, pointed ears, a forelock and strands of a goat beard. Examples below include (from left to right): <u>Left</u>: Pan mask uncovered at Hippos, Israel - In November 2014, the team at Antiochia Hippos, Israel, uncovered an extraordinary artifact—a large bronze mask of the Greek god Pan (or Faunus in the Roman pantheon). The mask depicts a young man with small horns on his head, a forelock, long pointed ears and strands of a goat beard. With glazed, furious eyes and a gaping mouth, the Pan mask appears to watch the passing world. Dr. Alexander Iermolin, the head conservator at the Zinman Institute of Archaeology at Haifa University, uncovered the Pan mask above a first-century C.E. floor while operating a metal detector in the basalt tower. Although the mask was not found *in situ* on the floor, it should also be dated to the first–second centuries C.E.[88] <u>Middle</u>: Pan mask posted on Google by Hemera Technologies. <u>Right</u>: Pan used in a European fountain.

<u>Conclusion</u>: Pan's appearance on the underside (trigger guard) of the Columbus gun can probably be attributed to Pan's symbolizing the god of fertile fields, groves, and wooded glens that Columbus claimed the New World had in abundance.

---

88   GREEK GOD PAN PARTIALLY CLEANED. Here the Pan mask from Hippos, Israel, is shown after its left half has been cleaned. After checking the results, the conservators cleaned and stabilized the rest of the mask. *Photo: M. Eisenberg. Michael Eisenberg, Director of the Hippos-Sussita Excavations, details this new discovery in* **"Pan at Hippos—Face of Greek God Unearthed,"** *published in the November/December 2015 issue of Biblical Archaeology Review. Weighing more than 11 pounds and measuring nearly 12 inches tall, the Pan mask is made of well-cast bronze. It was discovered outside the walled city of Hippos, Israel—in a basalt tower with 6.5-foot-wide exterior walls. Megan Sauter October 12, 2015. https://www.biblicalarchaeology.org/daily/biblical-sites-places/ biblical-archaeology-places/face-of-the-greek-god-pan/*

In addition, Pan was connected to the season of spring, the time of his equipping and planning his second voyage – and particularly the Spring of 1493, the likely time of his being gifted his gun.[89]

## MEDUSA HEADS ON COLUMBUS GUN

The Medusa heads on the Columbus gun appear on the octagonal part of the barrel in both of the two sets of silver-inlayed cartouches, or small heraldic medallions, that appear in two rows on each side of the Columbus motto. It is the top medallion in each set.

Today, the name Medusa conjures up images of a hideous, frightening monster with the snarling fangs of a snake and hair consisting of serpents. However, while this representation of Medusa

---

89    See previously referenced Navarrete documents re equipping the Second Voyage.

would have been familiar to an Ancient Greek or Roman, they also would have recognized another, more tame depiction of the famous gorgon. As Classical art evolved over time, the horrifying Medusa type slowly transformed into a type whose features recalled those of a beautiful woman. Her hair of snakes gave way to flowing curly locks. Occasionally, as in this example, she even sports a small pair of wings emerging from her head. The only reminder of her serpentine nature is the band below her chin that has been incised with diagonal lines recalling the texture of snake scales.[90]

Historically, before ancient Greece, Medusa was worshipped by the Libyan Amazons as a Serpent-Goddess, and associated with the destroyer aspect *Anath* (also known as *Athene*) of the Triple Goddess in North Africa and Crete. The name *Medusa* (*Medha* in Sanscrit, *Metis* in Greek and *Maat* in Egyptian) means "sovereign female wisdom."[91]

# OTHER EXAMPLES OF MEDUSA HEADS

In these examples, Medusa also sports a small pair of wings emerging from her head. Examples below include (from left to right): <u>Left</u>: This marble relief fragment, featuring the head of Medusa set on a clipeus (a round shield), was probably once originally part of a large sarcophagus. Here, Medusa's head is shown on a shield.[92] <u>Middle</u>: Bronze Furniture Attachment in shape of Medusa Head from ? Italy (1st c CE). Oval plaque with face surrounded by mass of snail-shell curls with hair strands articulated; at part in center bipartite wings with feathers articulated in outer portion rise diagonally to the sides.[93] <u>Right</u>: Medusa in a Roman mosaic tile floor in Andalusia, at the alcazar in Cordoba, Spain. Roman mosaic of head of medusa. It is in the Museu Naciona Arqueoligic in Tarragona, Spain.[94]

<u>Conclusion</u>: In addition to being an age-old mythical symbol used in Spain since Roman times, the Medusa head's appearance on the Columbus gun can best be explained in the Moorish and post-classical context as a woman of beauty and sovereign female wisdom, i.e. symbolizing Queen Isabella.

---

90   See: (CK.0046) Antiques.com
91   <u>Medusa in Greek Mythology</u> **compiled by Tracy Marks.** *http://www.windweaver.com/as/index.htm This online Medusa paper discusses the Libyan and Near Eastern conceptions of Medusa. www.perseus.tufts.edu.classes/finalp.html*
92   See: (X.0046) Antiques.com
93   Photograph: Neg: 3.21a. Wilcox Classical Museum. *The University of Kansas, Lawrence, Kansas 66045.*
94   F0029901 www.fotosearch.com

# HERALDIC EGGS ON THE BARREL

The Heraldic Eggs on the Columbus gun appear on the octagonal part of the barrel in both of the two sets of silver-inlayed cartouches, or small heraldic medallions, that appear in two rows on each side of the Columbus motto. They appear in both egg (oval) and round form. There are an astounding sixteen (16) of them in total.

It is obvious that every adornment on this gun either tells you explicitly what it is (e.g. Castle = Castile), or is a symbol or metaphor that stands for something else (e.g. Rabbit = Spain/Espana). So it is a natural question to ask: What are 16 eggs doing all over the barrel? There are two logical theories for their presence:

**THEORY NUMBER 1 - SPRINGTIME, FERTILITY & NEW LIFE:** This theory relies on the historical knowledge that the egg was widely used as a symbol of fertility, springtime, and renewal in antiquity and represented the start of new life, just as new life emerges from an egg when the chick hatches out.[95]

Since the beginning of time, Spring has been the season for new life. Eggs symbolized that new life in a real way. Eggs have so long been a part of the traditional celebrations of spring that there is no record of when the tradition actually began. Romans, Greeks, and Jews all used eggs in their springtime religious ceremonies and rituals.[96]

In Medieval Europe eggs were given as gifts to the servants. There is a story that in 1307 King Edward I had over 400 eggs dyed and covered with gold leaf and then presented them to the servants in his household.[97] Eggs as obvious fertility symbols feature prominently in the illuminated portrait of the

---

95  *David Leeming (2005). The Oxford Companion to World Mythology. Oxford University Press. p. 111. Retrieved 10 March 2013. For many, Easter is synonymous with fertility symbols such as the Easter Rabbit, Easter Eggs, and the Easter lily*

96  See: Marye Audet on Hubpages.com/easter-eggs

97  Ibid.

# THEORY NO. 1 - SYMBOLIC EGGS OF THE CATHOLIC KINGS[98]

**THEORY NUMBER 2 - RECALLS ONE OF THE BEST KNOWN STORIES IN THE LIFE OF COLUMBUS: "THE EGG OF COLUMBUS."** An egg of Columbus or Columbus' egg (Italian: uovo di Colombo) refers to a brilliant idea or discovery that seems simple or easy only after the fact. The expression refers to a story, dating from at least the 15th century, in which it is said that

---

98    Ferdinand & Isabella, youthful, but dignified early in their marriage, hold each other in their arms surrounded by egg fertility symbols. From a 1484 legal patent in the library of the University of Valladolid; MAS, as illustrated in McKendrick, page 29.

Christopher Columbus, having been told that finding a new trade route was inevitable and no great accomplishment, challenged his critics to make an egg stand on its tip. After his challengers give up, Columbus does it himself by tapping the egg on the table to flatten its tip. The Egg of Columbus has come to mean an amazingly simple solution for solving a heretofore difficult problem.

The Columbus Egg story seems to have originated with Italian historian and traveler Girolamo Benzoni in his book *History of the New World*, published in 1565.[99] It has been repeated by almost every Columbus scholar though centuries down to Washington Irving,[100] Samuel Elliot Morrison and others.

## THEORY NO. 2 - COLUMBUS BREAKING THE EGG BY WILLIAM HOGARTH, CIRCA 1750-60.[101]

99    Girolamo Benzoni (1572[1565]), *Historia del Mondo Nuovo*, Venice, pp. 12–3; English translation: *History of the New World by Girolamo Benzoni*, Hakluyt Society, London, 1857, page 17.

100    Washington Irving's *Life and Adventures of Christopher Columbus* (1828), Book V, Chapter 7, where it is used to applaud the explorer's "practical sagacity."

101    Wikipedia contributors. (2019, November 11). Columbus Breaking the Egg. In *Wikipedia, The Free Encyclopedia*. Retrieved 20:07, October 23, 2020, from https://en.wikipedia.org/w/index.php?title=Columbus_Breaking_the_Egg&oldid=925646686

However, it is the details of the egg incident that provide an important historical cross-reference that supports this author's opinion that the Columbus gun was made for him in the Spring of 1493. It is indeed an amazing coincidence that the exact time of the egg incident occurred in the spring of 1493 -- those same few months in the spring of 1493 that Columbus was in Barcelona celebrating his triumphant return from his First Voyage and getting ready for the Second Voyage. Author and historian, Arnold Garr, recounts the important details of the egg incident:[102]

"Christopher Columbus was certainly at a high point in his life when he returned from his first voyage to the Americas and was honored by King Ferdinand and Queen Isabella. He remained with the royal court at Barcelona for several weeks thereafter. During this time he advised the crown on diplomatic matters, made plans for a second transatlantic voyage, interviewed people who wished to sail to the New World, and attended royal social functions (Morison 2:14).

One of the most significant and memorable events that the Admiral attended at this time was . . . . a magnificent banquet given by Don Pedro Gonzales de Mendoza, Archbishop of Toledo and Grand Cardinal of Spain. Mendoza was a powerful and loyal supporter of the crown, and was probably the most important man in Spain after the king. On this night, the Cardinal had Columbus seated at the place of honor and treated him with ceremonial custom usually reserved for royalty; this meant that every dish served to the Admiral was first tasted by Mendoza, himself, and was then passed, with a cover, to Christopher.[103]

It was also at this auspicious occasion that the oft-repeated "egg incident" was supposed to have taken place. This anecdote is perhaps the best-known tale told about Columbus. As the story goes, during the party a jealous Spanish nobleman, attempting to minimize Christopher's accomplishments, approached the Admiral, and said: "Senor Cristobal, even if you had not undertaken this great enterprise, we should not have lacked a [Spaniard] who would have made the same discovery that you did" (Morison 2:15).

Columbus said nothing in reply, but instead placed an egg on the table and challenged all the men present to make the egg stand on its end by itself, without the aid of salt, crumbs or any other support. When everyone failed and the egg returned to Christopher, he tapped it on the table slightly crushing one end of the shell, then stood it on the crushed end with no props. The message of this simple demonstration was that when someone shows you how to break beyond self-imposed limits, anyone else can copy the great feat, but it takes a person of vision, courage, and determination to do something that has never before been done. (Morison 2:15).

Regarding the egg story, the famous American historian and writer, Washington Irving, claimed that the "universal popularity of this anecdote is proof of its merit," but others have concluded that the account might be apocryphal (Morison 2:15)."

---

102   Arnold K. Garr, *Christopher Columbus A Latter-Day Saint Perspective*, (Provo, Utah: Religious Studies Center, Brigham Young University, 1992), 53–62.

103   Author's note: Not only was Mendoza close to Queen Isabella, but he had long been one of Columbus' greatest supporters and advocates at the Royal Court.

# Christopher Columbus during a dinner at Cardinal Mendoza in 1493: "Columbus and his Egg," by Leo Reiffenstein, Artist.[104]

COLUMBUS AND HIS EGG.

Overall Conclusions:

Theory Number 1 - In addition to being an age-old mythical symbol of fertility and springtime (the time of preparing for Columbus' Second Voyage and likely presentation of this gun), the egg also represented the fertility and new life that was found in Columbus' New World.

---

104 Published in Vol. 1 of <u>Character Sketches of Romance, Fiction and the Drama</u>, A Revised American Edition of the Readers Handbook, by the Rev. E. Cobham Brewer. New York, 1892. Four Volumes.

<u>Theory Number 2</u> - Thus, we have the February-to-April, 1493 period of the egg event occurring within the same time frame that this author points to as the time of the probable making of the Columbus Gun. It seems likely that since the Columbus Egg story probably circulated like wildfire around the Royal Court, that the eggs were made as part of the gun's décor. In fact, it is a possibility that Don Pedro Gonzales de Mendoza, who hosted Columbus during this time may have actually overseen the making of the Columbus gun for Isabella, just as he had done overseeing the army and financing the final siege of Grenada.[105] Indeed, Mendoza had been in the Alhambra in 1492, which became an armory, and almost certainly must have had personal knowledge of the other 50 Espingoles stored there that were designated for Columbus' Second Voyage, also during this same time frame. In fact, Mendoza might have even originally ordered and paid for them as part of his financing of the final battle for Grenada.

Mendoza was more than just a religious figure. He was a warrior and fought in the battles of the Reconquista. During the Conquest of Granada, Don Pedro financially supported the Spanish army's conquest of Granada.[106] Upon its surrender on January 2, 1492 he occupied the town in the name of the Catholic sovereigns. Though his life was worldly, and though he was more soldier and statesman than priest, the "Great Cardinal", as he was commonly called, did not neglect his duty as a bishop. He used his influence with the queen and also at Rome to arrange a settlement of the disputes between the Spanish sovereigns and the papacy. He was also one of the few great men of Spain who had been an early and strong advocate of Christopher Columbus's cause.[107] Some historians have even speculated that Mendoza may have even been among those who contributed to the financing of Columbus's First Voyage.

Although Theory Number 1 provides the eggs a legitimate reason for being on the Barrel, this author comes down in favor of Theory Number 2 because it would be an unlikely historical coincidence that the timing of the "egg incident" at Cardinal Mendoza's dinner occurs during the same few months as this author believes that the Columbus gun was made for him -- in the Spring of 1493.

Thus, the details of the egg incident support an important historical cross-confirmation that this egg incident occurred during the same narrow time frame as the likely manufacture of the Columbus Gun -- the spring of 1493. Each element of the theory supports the other.


## CORNUCOPIA: THE HORN OF PLENTY

The Horn of Plenty, or Cornucopia, appears on the Columbus Gun as the flashpan attached to the lock plate.

---

105    Pedro González de Mendoza https://turtledove.fandom.com/wiki/Pedro_Gonz%C3%A1lez_de_Mendoza
106    Ibid.
107    *Herbermann, Charles, ed. (1913). "Pedro Gonzalez de Mendoza". Catholic Encyclopedia. New York: Robert Appleton Company.*

The cornucopia, or horn of plenty, is a time-honored symbol of abundance, inexhaustible riches and plenty; and it became associated with several deities, especially Tyche (Roman: Fortuna), the goddess of fortune, riches and abundance.

Definition: The cornucopia or cornu Copiae is, literally, the horn of plenty.[108]

The word 'cornucopia' actually dates back to the 5th century BC. It derives from two Latin words: "cornu," meaning horn (as in the name of that one-horned creature, the "unicorn") and "copia," meaning plenty (a relative of such words as "copious" and "copy"). Thus, "cornucopia" literally means horn of plenty, and the names are used interchangeably. It was usually depicted as a curved goat's horn, filled to overflowing with fruit and grain, but could actually have been filled with whatever the owner wished, and from then on, the horn - or cornucopia - became a symbol of plenty and whoever had it in his or her possession would never starve.[109]

Conclusion: The meaning of the cornucopia on the Columbus gun is one of the most obvious of all the many heraldic symbols adorning the gun. It stands for the abundance of inexhaustible riches and plenty to be found in the New World that Columbus displayed to the Spanish monarchs in the spring of 1493: gold, colorful parrots, fruits, vegetables, tobacco, native Caribbean Indians, and many other things never-before-seen in the Old World.

## SUN AND MOON SYMBOLS ON THE BARREL

The SUN and MOON SYMBOLS on the Barrel appear on the top of the barrel, beginning after it ceases to be octagonal and becomes rounded all the way up to the muzzle. Both symbols are engraved by the same hand that engraved all the other silver-inlaid/incised engravings of the Columbus Motto and other floral embellishments on the barrel.

---

108   See: <u>Ancient Rome Glossary</u> at <u>http://ancienthistory.about.com/library/bl/bl_dict_roman.htm</u>
109   Image of Radiant Cornucopia - October 2005 FSN Newsletter. Radiant Cornucopia.

Left: The SUN IN SPLENDOUR. The Sun in heraldry stands for power, glory and splendor. Bright, sparkling, in magnificence. Same as "Scintillant" and "Splendor".

Right: The MOON. The moon in heraldry is shown as a crescent and is the Deference for a second sun. It is the symbol for serene power and the sea. Same as "Lune"[110]

---

110    The Bingham Collection: A Pictorial Dictionary of Medieval Heraldry, Armour, Arms, Equipment, Clothes and Myths. Date of publication unknown.

# Examples of early 16th century Spanish sun and moon images:[111]

<u>Conclusion</u>: In addition to being age-old symbols used in Spain since Roman times, the Sun and Moon's appearance on the Columbus gun can best be explained in Renaissance context as symbolizing the serene power, glory and splendor of Columbus' sponsor, Queen Isabella.

## WITCH'S KNOT ON THE BREACH OF THE BARREL

The Witch's Knots on the Columbus gun appear on the octagonal part of the barrel in both of the two sets of silver-inlayed cartouches, or small heraldic medallions, that appear in two rows on each side of the Columbus motto. They are forward of the front sight in between two unknown pillar-like symbols. Both symbols are engraved by the same hand that engraved all the other silver-inlaid/incised engravings of the Columbus Motto and other floral embellishments on the barrel.

---

111    Sun and moon pictures: McKendrick, Melveena, <u>Ferdinand and Isabella</u>, New York, 1968, Page 48, crediting: a woodcut illustrated in a 1534 history of Aragon's rulers, in Tomish, <u>Historias...dels Reys de Arago</u>, 1534, New York Public Library.

The Witches knot is a symbol that is used to protect the bearer against negative witchcraft. The symbol would have been etched into people's doors, other possessions and worn as jewelry to protect themselves against malicious spells. Despite the name and the negative thoughts that surround the symbol, it is not an evil emblem at all.[112]

The symbol has also been used in weather charms by sailors. It is said that witches are able to create circles of protection, and to bind things magically, control the winds, raise storms, and influence

---

112   The Bingham Collection: <u>A Pictorial Dictionary of Medieval Heraldry, Armour, Arms, Equipment, Clothes and Myths</u>. Date of publication unknown.

the weather by tying knots in cords, or even in their own hair. It is also a symbol of protection against malevolent witchcraft. The interlacement represents the feminine control of the forces of nature.

The circle is one of the primary female symbols representing the sacred or consecrated space. Possibly due to having to be engraved in tight quarters, this example is missing the inner circle.

The spirals form the sign of the serpent. The serpent is the oldest symbol of female energy, the embodiment of enlightenment and wisdom. This combination of cogent symbols makes the Witches Knot a representation of female might and power.

Conclusion: The Witch's Knots appearance on the Columbus gun can best be explained in the Renaissance context as symbolizing a representation of female might and power. Since the symbol has also been used in weather charms by sailors to control the winds, raise or calm storms, and influence the weather, they can be interpreted as goodwill weather blessings from Columbus' sponsor, Queen Isabella.

## OTHER LEONARDO "FINGERPRINTS" ON THE COLUMBUS GUN

As previously stated, with its gold and silver decorations and its chiseled steel sculptural décor, the Columbus Gun is just as much a work of art as it is a solidly constructed weapon of war.

However, in addition to its Automatic-Opening Pan Cover Mechanism having been designed by Da Vinci, much of the gun's artistic décor seems to have his fingerprints all over it as well. Let's take a look:

## SIX DA VINCI-STYLE DRAGONS

For example, as has been shown, there are six dragons adorning the gun, and these look to be distinctively Da Vinci-style dragons.

**The first dragon is on the lock plate and its head is holding the end of the Horn of Plenty flashpan. The second dragon is the serpentine match holder. The third dragon is the tiller trigger. The fourth dragon is on the bottom of the stock facing the rabbit.**

**The fifth and sixth dragons appear on the backplate of the lock.**

Note the shape of the wings, corkscrew tail and the shape of the head with its projecting tongue and feathered head back – all features that are found on Da Vinci-style dragons.

Below is Da Vinci's famous drawing of the Dragon Striking Down Lion.[113] Note the similarities.

113  Illustration: Courtesy of LeonardoDaVinci.net. https://www.leonardodavinci.net/dragon-striking-down-lion.jsp#prettyPhoto

**Left: Da Vinci's famous drawing of the 7-Headed Dragon.**[114] **Da Vinci's Dragon from his "Bestiary" drawing.**[115] **Note the similarities to the dragons on the Columbus gun.**

It is known through accounts from Giorgio Vasari and Anonimo Gaddiano that Leonardo made painted shields with dragons on them as early as 1472. One was supposedly sold by Ser Piero da Vinci to merchants and eventually to the Duke of Milan.[116] Albeit, none of these has survived to modern times. Another Leonardo shield story Vasari is recounted that concerns his "pet" dragon.[117]

---

114    The British Museum. Museum number: 1946,0713.243.

115    Royal Collection Trust / © Her Majesty Queen Elizabeth II 2019.

116    List of works by Leonardo da Vinci From Wikipedia

117    Leonardo da Vinci's Pet Dragon. Posted on May 5, 2008 by 100swallows https://100swallows.wordpress.com/2008/05/05/leonardo-da-vincis-pet-dragon/

One day Leonardo da Vinci's dad knocked on his door. "Haven't you finished that shield yet? The guy's been waiting for it for over two months?" Leonardo called from deep inside his room. "Just a minute!"

Not even his dad had ever entered. It was a wizard's workshop and contained secrets. "All right! Come in."

"Ugh!" said his dad, wincing as he walked in. "Stinks like the devil in here. Don't you smell.....?"

And then he let go a howl of fear. "What is THAT?" His eyes were fixed on a strange monster wriggling in a corner of the room. It looked like no animal on earth—in fact, it looked like a dragon. "Fine," said Leonardo, who had been watching his father's reaction. He walked over to the monster, picked it up, and handed it to his dad. "You can take it now—I see that it works."

It was a monster he had painted on the buckler, snarling and threatening, looking so real his father had been frightened. "Incredible!" his dad said, beginning to smile. "How did you make it?"

Leonardo opened the shutters of the only window in the room and let light fill the room. There on his work-table were the bodies and parts of bodies of a dozen animals. "I make my own monsters," Leonardo explained. "I took the scales from this carp and the wings and teeth from this huge bat and the crest from this rooster and I glued them onto the body of the lizard here. I thought he needed a longer tail too, so I used this snake. When he was all assembled and propped up, I painted him on the shield. Before you came in here I set it up in the half-light to see if you would think it was real, and you did, so I'm satisfied. I hope your friend who ordered the buckler will like it."

**Not every renaissance artist made their dragons the same way. Da Vinci's dragons were quite different from his contemporary, Michelangelo's dragons (as is shown below in Michelangelo's "The Torment of Saint Anthony."[118]**

Note that Michelangelo's dragons are more short-necked, spiny, fishlike creatures, often with squid-like wings seen on the lower-right dragon.

---

118   Courtesy: Kimbell Art Museum.

**Albrecht Durer - The Revelation of St John, 10. The Woman Clothed with the Sun and the Seven-headed Dragon.**[119]

Note this Durer dragon, circa 1497, also differs from the Da Vinci and Michelangelo's dragons with its horse-shaped heads, prominent, and sometimes forward-facing horns, and smooth unscaled tail.

---

119   Private Collection of Staatliche Kunsthalle Karlsruhe. Photo Christies Images via The Bridgeman Art Library.

# RABBIT VS. DRAGON: ANOTHER "QUADRUPED VS. AVIAN" FACEOFF – LEONARDO'S ALLEGORY OF BOAT, WOLF, AND EAGLE

The Allegorical drawing of the Boat, Wolf, and Eagle,[120] represents another of Da Vinci's "Quadruped vs. Avian" allegorical face-offs. The boat sails toward a globe surmounted by a crowned eagle.[121] The drawing, which is at Windsor, was probably made for the wedding of Giuliano de Medici to Philiberta of Savoy. It is another example of Leonardo's taste for the fantastic, which he never lost despite the strong rational core of his temperament.[122]

LeonardoDaVinci.net's interpretation of the allegorical drawing is:

> "The extraordinary symbolism of the picture might also refers to the wolf as the Church, which is in charge of the boat with its living tree and compass. Does it suggest that the wolf - a rather negative image for the Church - is given too much direction over the life of man? The Pope and German Emperor were rivals for power at this time, and in Italy the great families and political leaders were divided between two. The shinning eagle may suggest that the Emperor is a leading light in the world. And why is the Church sailing towards the land and what is, presumably, the German Empire? Either way, it is not difficult to second guess where Leonardo's own sympathies lay."

---

120  Illustration: Courtesy of LeonardoDaVinci.net. https://www.leonardodavinci.net
121  Author's Note: This is a single-headed eagle of St. John style, not the later double-headed eagle of Carlos V, Burgundy, etc.
122  Illustration: Courtesy of LeonardoDaVinci.net. https://www.leonardodavinci.net

LeonardoDaVinci.net's interpretation is based on the false premise that the eagle represents the German Hapsburg Empire, whereas Abenaim explains it as Columbus (Wolf of the Sea) sets his course toward the crowned Eagle of St. John, representing Queen Isabella.[123]

<u>Conclusion</u>: Fortunately, in the case of the "Quadruped vs. Avian" faceoff of the Rabbit vs. the Dragon on the Columbus Gun, an interpretation is easily forthcoming due to their obvious context on Columbus' gun symbolizing his/Spain's conquest over the Sea of Darkness, as represented by the dragon.

## POMEGRANATE - DRAWING OF A BOTANICAL STUDY BY LEONARDO DA VINCI

Among the major innovations of the Renaissance, and no doubt the most far-reaching in its impact, was the rehabilitation or rediscovery of nature as a positive entity. Indeed, according to one Venetian scholar, the Renaissance made nature its religion, "sought God in nature." For Leonardo, rational knowledge was based on the experience of the senses: man's role was to observe nature as attentively and completely as possible.[124]

---

123    Abenaim, pages 24 – 25.
124    Illustration: <u>Courtesy of LeonardoDaVinci.net</u>. <u>https://www.leonardodavinci.net</u>

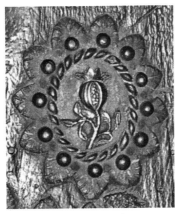

Conclusion: Da Vinci's sketches of the pomegranate in the plant and animal world suggest his love and respect for the works of nature, rather than any known connection of his pomegranates to heraldry or the Granada coat of arms and subsequent adoption into the shield of the Catholic Kings. Nevertheless it would be a mistake not to note his interest in capturing it in his other artworks.


## LEONARDO'S MEDUSA HEADS

In examining and comparing the Medusa Head on the Columbus Gun with other Leonardo Medusa Heads, it should be noted that Italian parade shields in Renaissance times often displayed a Medusa Head on them.[125]

Left: One of the Medusa Heads on the Columbus Gun. Right: A 1597 purported copy or version of Leonardo's Medusa shield by Caravaggio.[126]

---

125   In his *Vita di Leonardo* (1568), Vasari reports that, as a very young man, Leonardo represented the head of Medusa on a wooden shield.

126   Caravaggio's version of the subject, 1597. His purported indebtedness to Leonardo's early work remains problematic. *Medusa* is either of two paintings attributed by Giorgio Vasari to Leonardo da Vinci. Neither painting survives.

Leonardo Da Vinci's Lost Paintings of Medusa Heads on Shields:

"Medusa's Shield has been lost in time but is one of those mysterious Leonardo da Vinci works with a high level of spirit and debate. Originally painted in his youth an art historian Giorgio Vasari made the account in 1550 that the painting was so realistic it frightened both Leonardo's father as well as others. It was seen as associated with death and was secretly sold to merchants.

Vasari indicates that the face was painted on a wooden shield cut from fig trees. It was a favor to a peasant friend of his who fashioned the shield. Leonardo in his experimental style took the shield and heated it by fire and made it smooth. He then moved to make one his very first masterpieces.

When his father Ser Piero came to see the shield and knocked on the door, Leonardo told him to wait. He took the painting and adjusted it near a window with the soft light peering through. Ser Piero came in and took a look at the painting and stepped back with a gasp. Leonardo said, "This work serves the end for which it was made; take it, then, and carry it away, since this is the effect that it was meant to produce."

It is believed that the painting made its way to the Duke of Milan who held it for a while and then sold it again for 3X what he paid for it. Medusa was part of Greek Mythology. She was seen as a protector who was sexually forced by Poseidon and in Athena's rage she took the "fair cheeked Medusa" and turned her hair into snakes and her skin into scales so that all men would hate her. Her very look would turn a man to stone."[127]

<u>Conclusion</u>: Although some art historians have doubted the veracity of this anecdote, Leonardo's shield (long since lost) has been said to inspire several early 17th-century painters who may have seen it in the collection of Ferdinand I de Medici. Rubens and Caravaggio are known to have painted their own versions of the subject, but their indebtedness to Leonardo's painting (assuming they had seen it) is uncertain.[128]

# SWIVEL YOKE ON COLUMBUS GUN IS ALSO PICTURED IN THE SAME DA VINCI'S MADRID CODICES THAT PICTURES THE UNIQUE LOCK MECHANISM

Staffs with yokes for supporting the barrel and assist in aiming it appear in the late 15th century. More remarkable, however, is the more than coincidental appearance of a fixed swivel yoke in the same MADRID CODICES of Da Vinci that also illustrates his Automatic Opening Pan Cover Lock ignition system.

---

127   See - Thursday, October 3, 2013: http://www.academic-capital.net/2013/10/leonardo-di-vincis-lost-painting.html
128   From Wikipedia, the free encyclopedia. (Redirected from Medusa (Leonardo da Vinci))

As can be seen from the preceding photo, the early 16th century hacabuche was a monstrous hand-gun, often measuring over 5ft. and weighing a back-breaking 30-35 pounds! Due to its tremendous weight, it made a great rampart, or wall gun, gun as well as an infantry gun.

Their heavy barrels were possibly supported by and fired from a fork, although Lavin finds that these forks: "neither appear listed among the equipment of foot soldiers nor depicted in contemporary illustrations prior to the seventeenth century."[129] However, other 16th and 17th century European sources show the contemporary and abundant use of forks (see Maximillian Codex illustrations, etc.).

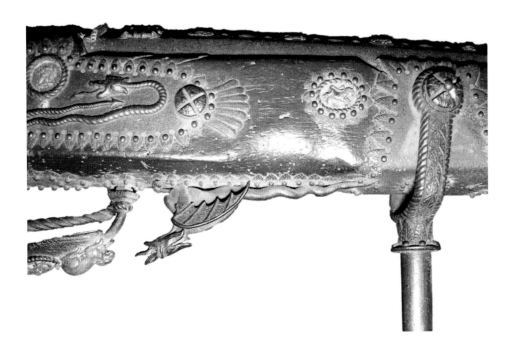

---

129    Lavin, page 44, referencing his footnote #12: Bernal Diaz del Castillo, *Historia verdadera de la conquista de Nueva Espana* (Mexico: Pedro Robredo, 1939), Vol. I, p.i 15. "According to an inspection of the* garrison of St, Augustine, Florida^ made on 27 September, 1578, the equipmentofanarcabucero consisted of an arquebus, sword, powder flask, and charges. Jeanette Thurber Conner (ed. and trans.), GolomatJ Records of Spanish Florida (Delarid: The Florida State Historical Society, 1930), Vol. II, p. 136.

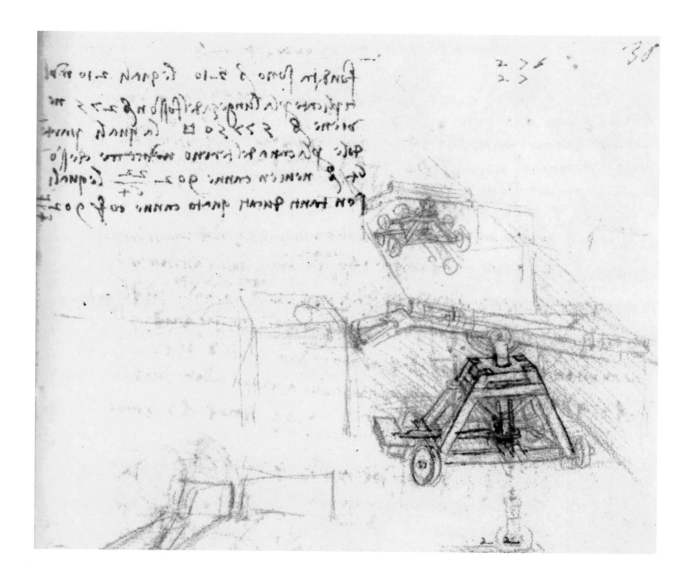

Conclusion: It would be folly to ignore that this important feature on the Columbus Gun is also pictured and described in the same MADRID CODICES that also picture and describe the gun's unique Automatic Opening Pan Cover Lock ignition system.[130]

## WAS COLUMBUS GOLD FROM FIRST VOYAGE USED TO ADORN THE DA VINCI/COLUMBUS GUN?

First of all, it is now thought that Columbus brought back more gold from his voyages than the gold-greedy Spaniards ever gave him credit for. For them, this foreigner could never find enough gold to satisfy them. Whatever the exact amount, we will never know, but we can surmise that there was likely more than enough to spare an ounce or two to adorn his gun.

---

130  MADRID CODICES, page 36.

Other known uses of gold from his First Voyage are as follows:

<u>COLUMBUS GOLD From First Voyage Used To Adorn Queen Isabella's Artworks -</u>

"It is said that Queen Isabella had an elegant Missal wrought with some of the grains of gold brought home from this first voyage. Great artists decorated it, and the Queen of Sheba, King Solomon and King David appeared therein with the faces and forms of the sovereigns then on the throne. She bequeath it to her grandson, Charles V, and it is still extant in the Royal Library at Madrid."[131]

<u>COLUMBUS GOLD Sent to the Pope -</u>

"It was resolved that Dr. Bei Nicolo de Carbajal, then Bishop of Cartagena, should be dispatched on an embassy to the Pope, with a present of some of the first gold brought from the Indies, and instructions to represent the vast consequences to Christianity that were likely to accrue from the new discoveries. Pope Alexander VI. was an Aragonese, and had been a subject of Ferdinand."[132]

There are five gold Lion Heads on the gun, each about ¼ inch in diameter. There is one on the lock plate, one on the lock's back plate, and three on the trigger guard, where they surround the "Rabbit vs. Dragon" sculptural adornment. In addition, the eyes of the Dragon are made with tiny gold eyeballs. These gold adornments are pictured below:

# One on the Lock Plate

---

131   Annie Randall White, <u>THE STORY OF COLUMBUS AND THE WORLDS COLUMBIAN EXPOSITION</u>, 1893, pages 136 – 139.
132   Markham. Clements R. (Clements Robert). Sir. 1830-1916. <u>Life of Christopher Columbus.</u> Philip & Son, London, January 1, 1892, page 137.

## One on the Lock's Back Plate

## Three on the Trigger Guard, where they Surround the "Rabbit vs. Dragon" Sculptural Adornment

# The Eyes of the Dragon are Made with Tiny Gold Eyeballs

## Gold Altar Gilded with the First Gold Brought Back from America by Columbus, at the Late Gothic Carthusian Monastery of Santa María de Miraflores, Burgos:

An extraordinary altarpiece and several stone funerary monuments within the fifteenth-century monastery church of Santa María de Miraflores in Burgos have just been unveiled following a two-year WMF-sponsored restoration. Located in northwestern Spain, the Cartuja (or Carthusian monastery) de Santa María de Miraflores was designed by Hans and Simon of Cologne and completed in 1482. The complex was built atop the remains of an early fifteenth-century hunting lodge that was given to the Carthusian Order by King John II in 1442 and which was subsequently gutted by fire. Within the monastery church is one of the most important ensembles of late Gothic art and architecture to survive in Spain—two intricately carved stone sepulchers and <u>a massive gilt and polychrome wooden altar—all the work of "wandering Jewish" artist Gil de Siloé, executed between 1493 and 1499</u>.[133]

Burgos, a city in Castilla-Leon situated in the Pilgrim's Road to Santiago de Compostela, still preserves important vestiges of its medieval splendor. The city, which was the capital of the unified kingdom of Castilla-Leon for five centuries, boasts a masterpiece of Spanish Gothic architecture: the cathedral of Burgos, declared World Heritage.[134]

<u>Conclusion</u>: There was amply enough gold from the First Voyage to have spared an ounce or two for the Columbus gun.

## COULD THESE GOLD LION HEADS POSSIBLY BE A SIGNATURE OF LEONARDO DA VINCI?

These five gold Lion Heads are not heraldic symbols for Queen Isabella's heraldic "Lion of Leon," for as we have seen on her Coat of Arms and on the Columbus Gun, that lion is in the pose known in heraldry as the "Lion Rampant," i.e. standing up, in profile, and with claws outstretched. Rather the gun shows us five simple gold lion faces from the frontal view, which was not common in heraldic use.

## Lion Rampants (Left) vs. Gold Lion Faces (Right)

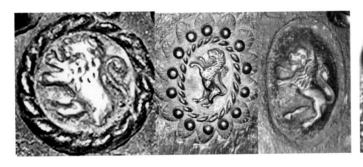 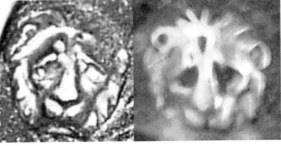

---

133    Angela M.H. Schuster and Holly Evarts, <u>Spanish Splendor Celebrating the Late Gothic at the Carthusian Monastery of Santa María de Miraflores,</u> ICON, Issue No.14, spring 2007, pages 10 – 14.

134    Read more: http://www.virtualtourist.com/travel/Europe/Spain/Castilla_y_Leon/Burgos-273266/Things_To_Do-Burgos-Monastery_of_Miraflores-BR-1.html#ixzz1guAgLeuZ

The silver Lion Ramparts shown above are from the Lock, Stock and Barrel, respectively. The gold Lion Faces are from the Lock and Trigger Guard, respectively.

## Leonardo used LIONS and Lion Symbols as a hidden signature for LEONARDO -

So what can these gold lion heads stand for? They can't all represent the same thing, otherwise there would be no need to have one of each type of lion on the lock plate. Abenaim states that Da Vinci used lions as his hidden signature on artworks he didn't want to be identified with for fear of persecution by the inquisition.

The impact of the Inquisition on art, literature and everyday life in those times cannot be underestimated. During a very long six centuries in time, even a chronicle couldn't be written, or a painting painted, without undergoing the scrutiny of the Inquisition. As ably described by Abenaim:

"If not very careful, even the author of a fable risked fueling a blazing pyre in a public square. Thus, creating a safer means of communication, by any stretch of the imagination, became a necessity in order to escape the claws of the censorship. In so doing, History was filled with tortuous lies to mask the facts deemed unbearable at face value."[135]

Leonardo Da Vinci was famous for a technique called "*sfumato*" which added a subliminal touch of realism to his paintings, but sometimes acted as a "fog" to conceal hidden meanings in them.[136] Examples of \

Seen paintings are as follows:

"*Old Man with Ivy Wreath and Lion's Head* (Leonardo Da Vinci) This is yet another self-portrait of the artist where he draws once again a lion *in lieu* of his identity in the lower right corner. Obviously, he has aged, lost his upper teeth, his upper jaw has caved in. Obviously Leonardo spends a lot of time, watching himself grow older and ugly in a mirror. There is a complete series of self-portraits offering the view of his aging process, which he must find interesting from a clinical point of view; if not from the narcissist complex he had developed in his youth, when '*he was young and beautiful*'.[137]

---

135   Abenaim, page 6.
136   Ibid., page 8.
137   Ibid., page 51.

*Saint John-Baptist* (by Leonardo Da Vinci with Melzi's or Salai's participation):

"The pointing finger appears most particularly in this painting, whereby <u>the subject, mostly naked, wears a leopard skin. Leopard is another way to say Leo. This is his signature and a clever way to conceal his identity, since his paintings are destined to a religious order.</u> In the following painting, the religious connotation is even more audacious. His finger pointing parallel to the cross implicitly reveals that the subject is a believer in one God (Symbol of Judaism) and not in the Trinity symbolized by the cross in parallel lost in the dark background; we are in the days of the Inquisition and religion is taboo. However, Leonardo chooses to mock the Inquisitors and the church in his own [way]. . . ."[138,139]

---

138   Ibid., page 46.
139   Emphasis (underlining) added by author.

## DA VINCI - QUEEN ISABELLA - COLUMBUS: WHO KNEW WHO?

### Da Vinci:

WHO
KNEW WHO?

**Queen Isabella**

**Columbus**

# QUEEN ISABELLA ⟷ COLUMBUS:

1. The Queen and Columbus had a long-term relationship which spanned the many years that Columbus spent beseeching the Royal Court to sponsor his voyage of discovery to reach the East by sailing West.

2. Columbus, Beatriz Galindo and His Female Friends at the Royal Court:

"Columbus did not limit his affections exclusively to men. Even among the so-called weaker sex, he had admirers. A good conversationalist, he had to enliven many of the dialogues of noblemen's wives or of government officials whom he literally chased to get their signatures on requisite documents, as well as the women who were a part of Queen Isabella's inner circle. Thus it was clear that women of many backgrounds supported him with their friendship. Despite his constant visits to Gaspar de Gricio, the royal secretary did not seem to condemn his horrible Latin and Columbus had much contact with his sister, Beatriz Galindo, instructor of classical languages to Queen Isabella. Beatriz could very well have consulted with Columbus on how he could correct his questionable language skills."[140]

3. Columbus Fought alongside Isabella at the Siege of Baza, 1489:

"The year 1489 was a hazardous but fruitful one. The sovereigns were pushing vigorously their conquest of the Moor. Isabella herself attended the army, and may have appeared in the beleaguering lines about Baza, in one of those suits of armor which are still shown to travelers. Zuñiga says that Columbus arrayed himself among the combatants . . . ."[141]

4. COLUMBUS was at the SURRENDER of GRANADA in 1492:

". . . . while I was occupied at Madrid in writing the Life of Columbus. In searching for traces of his early life I was led among the scenes of the war of Granada, he having followed the Spanish sovereigns in some of their campaigns, and been present at the surrender of the Moorish capital.[142]

---

140 Consuelo Varela, CHRISTOPHER COLUMBUS and The Mystery of The Bell of the Santa Maria, White Star Publishers, Vercelli, Italy, 2008, Page 43.
141 JUSTIN WINSOR, CHRISTOPHER COLUMBUS AND HOW HE RECEIVED AND IMPARTED THE SPIRIT OF DISCOVERY, BOSTON AND NEW YORK, HOUGHTON, MIFFLIN AND COMPANY, The Riverside Press, Cambridge, 1891, [The Project Gutenberg Ebook # 42059 of Christopher Columbus and How He Received and Imparted the Spirit of Discovery by Justin Winsor], Page 170.
142 Washington Irving, Chronicle of the Conquest of Granada, Sunnyside, 1850, following the narrative of William H. Prescott in The History of the Reign of Ferdinand and Isabella the Catholic, (1837). Prescott specialized in late Renaissance Spain and the early Spanish Empire. https://www.gutenberg.org/files/3293/3293-h/3293-h.htm#link2H_INTR

# DA VINCI ←——————→ QUEEN ISABELLA:

According to Renaissance historian and biographer Jacques Abenaim, what little we know about Da Vinci's life is derived from Vasari and is either not corroborated, or demonstrably false:

> "Inevitably, in view of Leonard Da Vinci's life and works, the question which begs an answer is: what part of his life did the biographer Vasari improvise when he wrote *"The lives of the artists"* . . . . This thesis raises many questions about Vasari's erroneous testimonials."[143]

> "As to the rest of his biography, Vasari didn't corroborate the majority of his allegations. The fact being, he wrote Leonardo Da Vinci's 50 years after the master had died, and we know too well how facts can be distorted over such lapses of time. For example, Vasari had never seen the portrait of Mona Lisa when he called the subject "Giaconda"; he stated affirmatively: *"she was Sforza's mistress"*. Unfortunately, nobody of knowledge was alive to contradict him."[144]

In addition, Abenaim states that Da Vinci spent a good portion of his life in Spain:

> " Did Christopher Columbus and Leonardo Da Vinci undergo the same treatment? Perhaps they did, but what remains shocking about both characters is that they've spent the best part of their lives together in Spain, but that important fact has been completely ignored."[145]

Abenaim also suggests that it is possible Leonardo put to use his formidable weaponry concepts in a covert military operation in Spain during the battle for Grenada:

> "Adversely, Vasari claims that in 1480 *'Leonardo went to Venice, where he put his talent to work in the eventuality of a Turkish invasion'.* The fact is, immediately upon their arrival in Spain; the Austrians managed with the Spaniards to build enormous towers, portable bridges, and successfully bombarded the walls of Malaga, the last stronghold before Granada; exactly as per Leonardo's description of war concepts described earlier in the letter addressed to Sforza."[146]

This above quote from Abenaim reminds us of the previously discussed "LEONARDO the Arms Merchant -Have Guns Will Travel" - The letter to Ludovico:

In 1482, Leonardo moved to Milan, where he was employed for nearly twenty years by the Duke, Ludovico Sforza. In the letter offering his services to the Duke, Leonardo made much of his technical skills. In his words: "I know how, when a place is besieged, to make endless variety of bridges, and covered chariots and ladders. Again, I have kind of mortars easy to

---

143 Jacques Abenaim, <u>DA VINCI's SFUMATO - The Revelation – Book I - Essay</u> Legal registration in Canada ISBN 978-0-9812591-1-6, page 7.
144 Ibid., page 11.
145 Ibid., page 4.
146 Ibid., page 24.

carry; and with these I can fling small stones almost resembling a storm. And if the fight should be at sea I have kinds of many machines most efficient for offence and defense; and vessels which will resist the attack of the largest guns. I will make covered chariots, safe and unattackable, which there is no body of men so great but they would break them. In case of need I will make big guns and mortars of fine and useful forms, out of the common type. I would contrive catapults and other machines."

The Diaries and Letters of Beatriz Galindo:

Beatriz Galindo - *La Latina* (1474-1534) was a Salamanca University professor who was a Spanish Latinist and educator. She was a writer, humanist and a teacher of Queen Isabella of Castile and her children. She was one of the most educated women of her time. She was nicknamed La Latina for her skill in Latin, and was appointed tutor to the children of Queen Isabella of Castile. She also taught Catherine of Aragon, the future wife of Henry VIII of England, and Joanna of Castile, the future wife of Philip of Habsburg and later known as Juana the Mad.[147] She was adamant about Leonardo Da Vinci's relationship with Queen Isabella and about his presence in Spain. Beatriz Galindo wrote:

"University of Salamanca, April 20, 1503 Without Queen Isabella's support, I probably wouldn't be a professor at the University of Salamanca. (…) Being the only female professor among a faculty of men, I am constantly undermined and tried. (…), whereas Leonardo has great regards for Isabella (…)"

"University of Salamanca, May 21, 1503. This late afternoon, they gather at the faculty of Advance Studies for the final touch ups on the painting. When all the students are gone, the courtyard of the faculty becomes the quietest place on the campus. Da Vinci must have chosen this area because the courtyard is opened to the sky; the openness inspires him. Likewise, Queen Isabella feels relaxed; she can be herself at last. Here, I feel all emotions. Da Vinci can be the artist he is and Queen Isabella a woman relieved from the burden of her crown. I stand in the center of the courtyard admiring the architecture. To be walking on the lush grass, makes me feel like I am walking on a divine rug, too perfect to be man-made. The enclosure of the courtyard with the covered walkways surrounding us makes me feel caught up within the boundaries of my profession. But as I am drawn back to reality, I look up to the heavy pillars, head adorned and spires pointing towards the sky, as I am reminded of the infinite beauty of the sky; if I could stretch my arm a little further, I would plunge my fingers in an ocean of stars. Too bad, the initial background of the Court yard has been painted over. Da Vinci argues that the former background drew too much focus away from the subject. Now all that enhances his masterpiece is a blur of grassy landscape. Nevertheless, I love that portrait. It captures realistically Queen Isabella's glowing aura. Personally, I suspect Da Vinci is in love with the Queen, not necessarily the person, but the virtues she characterizes: sincerity, romanticism

---

147   The Biographical Dictionary of Women in Science by Marilyn Bailey Ogilvie and Joy Dorothy Harvey, Taylor & Francis 2000. ISBN 978-0-415-92039-1.

and affection. He is infatuated by her and he doesn't know it. He probably believes she is the perfect symbol of feminism."[148]

However, Vasari never once mentions Beatriz Galindo in his The Lives of the Artists. As Abenaim explains:

"No wonder why Vasari didn't breathe a word about Beatriz Galindo's testimonials; these letters were discovered only during the 19th century. Had Vasari known about the letters, he would have had to change his biography a third time. Instead, his biography had been largely accepted and Beatrix Galindo's letters were left unexplained. Although they give a whole new perspective to Leonardo Da Vinci's life and works, two letters could no longer justify a changed main stream. Yet, this shadow of light explains everything in Leonardo Da Vinci's life and works. Evidently, his own negligence didn't help the matter, but the fact remains; Leonardo Da Vinci was in Spain and for a long period of time."[149]

## DA VINCI ⟷ COLUMBUS:

The Project Gutenberg Ebook, The Notebooks of Leonardo Da Vinci, Volume 2 lays the groundwork for exploring whether or not there might have been a relationship between Da Vinci and Columbus via geographical convenience and coincidence of timing:[150]

"It is impossible now to decide whether Leonardo, when living in Florence, became acquainted in his youth with the doctrines of Paolo Toscanelli the great astronomer and mathematician (died 1482), of whose influence and teaching but little is now known, beyond the fact that he advised and encouraged Columbus to carry out his project of sailing round the world. His name is nowhere mentioned by Leonardo, and from the dates of the manuscripts from which the texts on astronomy are taken, it seems highly probable that Leonardo devoted his attention to astronomical studies less in his youth than in his later years."

Firstly, there is the Columbus Correspondence with Toscanelli regarding Sailing West to find the East:

"Toscanelli, at the time of writing this letter to Columbus, had long enjoyed a reputation as a student of terrestrial and celestial phenomena. He had received, in 1463, the dedication by Regiomontanus of his treatise on the quadrature of the circle. He was, as has been said, an old

---

148    Ibid., page 12. The author's added emphasis (underlining), highlights Beatriz Galindo's testimony that Da Vinci actually painted a "lost" portrait of Queen Isabella. Abenaim, among other have speculated that this lost portrait of Isabella is actually the Mona Lisa.
149    Ibid., page 13.
150    THE PROJECT GUTENBERG EBOOK, THE NOTEBOOKS OF LEONARDO DA VINCI, VOLUME 2. This eBook was produced by Charles Aldarondo and the Distributed Proofreaders team from a translation by Jean Paul Richter, 1888, XV -Astronomy. Release Date: January, 2004 [EBook #4999], page 856.

man of seventy-seven when Columbus opened his correspondence with him. It was not his fate to live long enough to see his physical views substantiated by Diaz and Columbus, for he died in 1482."[151]

Finally, there is the Columbus Correspondence with Da Vinci re Sailing West to find the East:

"It has been of late contended by H. Grothe, in his *Leonardo da Vinci* (Berlin, 1874), that it was at this time, too, when that eminent artist conducted a correspondence with Columbus about a western way to Asia. But there is little need of particularizing other advocates of a belief which had within the range of credible history never ceased to have exponents."[152]

---

151 JUSTIN WINSOR, <u>CHRISTOPHER COLUMBUS</u> <u>AND HOW HE RECEIVED AND IMPARTED THE SPIRIT OF DISCOVERY</u>, BOSTON AND NEW YORK, HOUGHTON, MIFFLIN AND COMPANY, The Riverside Press, Cambridge, 1891, [The Project Gutenberg Ebook # 42059 of Christopher Columbus and How He Received and Imparted the Spirit of Discovery by Justin Winsor], Page 117.

152 Ibid.

# COLUMBUS' Espingoles DOCUMENTATION of USE

## May, 1493 – Preparation for Second Voyage

- The Alcaide of Malaga ordered to furnish 50 "espingardas"
- The arsenal at the Alhambra ordered to furnish another 50
- Total of at least 100 on 2nd Voyage

The above 100 Espingoles/Espingardas were ordered for outfitting the Second Voyage in 1493:[153]

---

153  Don Martinez Fernandez De Navarrete, COLLECTION OF THE VOYAGES AND DISCOVERIES MADE BY THE SPANISH AT SEA SINCE THE END OF THE XV CENTURY, VOLUME II, SECOND EDITION, DOCUMENTS OF COLUMBUS AND OF THE FIRST POPULATIONS. By Order Of S.M. Madrid, Of The National Publishing House, 1859, page 54. This first translation from Spanish to English was commissioned by the author.

After Columbus had set sail on his Second Voyage there appears another 1493 order for guns recorded by Navarrete:[154]

"NUMBER LXXII. *[Messenger document from the King and Queen – September 1493]. Instructions that the Admiral gave Mosen Pedro Margarite to scope out the provinces of the Isle of Cuba.* (Legalized testimony in the Archive of the Indies in Sevilla, Leg. 5. Of Royal Decree.)

Item: by any experience that is had by this setting out on this land, some things are written below which are necessary to do: in everything, because you will be going to other provinces and places beyond those that have been experienced . . . . may you be very well informed and from this here city, all things that were needed by you will be sent you.

Firstly, ten and six on horse, and <u>two-hundred and fifty shield bearers and spearmen, and one-hundred and ten espingarderos (musketeers), and twenty Officers.</u>"[155]

# COLUMBUS' Espingoles

## January 30, 1495 – In Letter from Hispanola on Second Voyage:

- **Columbus orders 100 "espingardas" and "much ammunition" in a letter sent to Ferdinand & Isabella**

154 Ibid., page 126.
155 Emphasis (underlining) added by author.

In addition, there was an additional order for one hundred more espingardas requested in January, 1495, by Christopher Columbus along with a hundred cross-bows, two hundred cuirasses and "much ammunition."[156] This was obviously the armament to equip a company of two hundred infantry. It is also a definite indication of the equality the crossbow enjoyed with the handgun in the closing years of the fifteenth century.[157] In retrospect, in placing this order, Columbus was likely anticipating the forthcoming battle with the Taino Indians which took place a few weeks later in February. This epic Battle of Santo Cero will be discussed at length in Part II below.

**And finally, let's not forget those serpentine matchlock Espingoles that are so clearly pictured on the ramparts of the fort at Santo Domingo:**

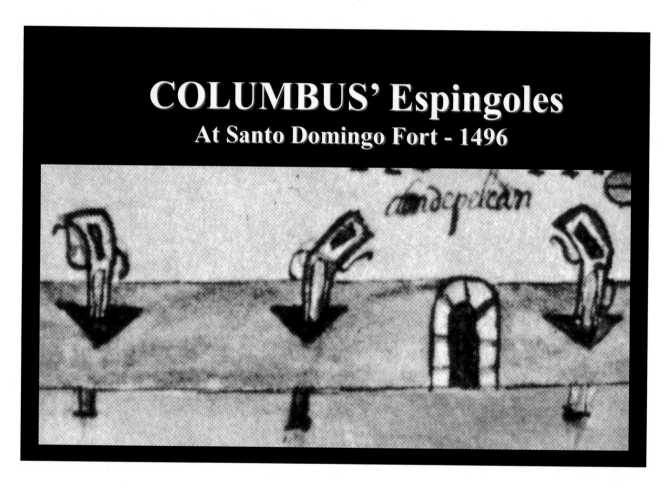

**COLUMBUS' Espingoles**
**At Santo Domingo Fort - 1496**

---

156  Cecil Jane (ed. and trans.), *Select Documents Illustrating the Four Voyage of Columbus* (London: Hakluyt Society, 1930), Vol. I. p. 107. Memorandum of Christopher Columbus sent to Fernando and Isabel by Antonio de Torres on 30 January, 1495.

157  Lavin page 43. Lavin uses "handguns" in his quote, rather than Espingoles, but in truth no one actually knows because all agree the terminology was used confusingly and interchangeably. This author come down on the side of some kind of serpentine matchlock, arquebus or espingole.

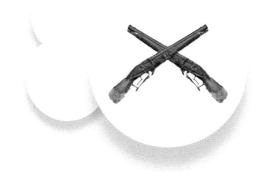

# PRIOR COMMENTARY ON THE COLUMBUS GUN

I n 1963 William Gilkerson published his epic work on firearms in the classical age of fighting sail, <u>BOARDERS AWAY II</u>. In "Section VIII – Little Artillery - ESPINGOLES AND MUSKE-TOONS," Gilkerson explains:

> "Espingoles and musketoons were the smallest members of the petit artillery family but their role was essentially the same as that of their weightier cousins. Like the swivel cannon and howitzers, they were primarily used as scatter guns, firing pistol balls or big lead pellets called "swan drops . .
>
> The word espingole was used to describe just about any swivel-mounted gun with a wooden shoulder-stock, no matter what the barrel style; its bore could be cylindrical throughout or cylindrical with a slight flare at the muzzle or conical or broadly flared with round or horizontally elliptical configuration.[158]

Gilkerson then goes on to comment specifically on the Columbus Gun:

> "Perhaps the earliest-known espingole with fixed swivel is a heavy, iron-barrel gun that appears to have originated in the 1500s, although it is difficult to date with any precision because the venerable gun bears features suggesting two or more time periods and markings associating it in some way to the name of Christopher Columbus. This espingole is illustrated and detailed in Plate V. with its swivel yoke still attached to an extremely early style of stock which has lost its butt-end to worm damage. Judging from its originally concave comb, apparently the butt once formed a heavy "fish-tail" profile. As is, the weapon measures 50' in length overall and weighs 50 pounds.
>
> This provocative relic's full investigation beckons further scholarship; it is possible to afford it only the most cursory treatment here, and that by courtesy of its owner, Norman Flayderman.

---

158   William Gilkerson, <u>BOARDERS AWAY II</u>, Andrew Mowbray, Inc., Lincoln-Rhode Island-USA, 1993, page 97.

He notes its measurements and describes its decoration as including: "Numerous small solid gold and silver inlays on all lock parts and some similar gold and silver work on the furniture. Numerous large silver inlays along the top of the barrel in shape of rampant lions, eagle, human heads. The large silver plaque at the wrist bears a huge crest of the royal house of Spain (castle and lion, etc.). [85]

The barrel is octagonal at its breech, and the top flat is inscribed with inlaid silver characters spelling: "POR CASTILLA Y POR LEON NUEVO MUNDO HALLO COLON," which roughly translates "For Castille and Leon the New World Was Found by Columbus," a motto that appears on the Columbus coat of arms. Its presence on the barrel of this espingole is enigmatic. The barrel inscription is of distinctly more primitive workmanship than most of the other decorative work, suggesting the gun's most florid embellishments as of later vintage. It is unlikely its matchlock was original to the gun, which appears to have begun life as a simple 16th-century shoulder-stocked cannon (perhaps with no lock at all) of a type that conceivably could have been known to Columbus but would have been more familiar a generation or two later. . . . Pending further research, probably in Spain, all is speculative regarding the story of this extremely early espingole."[159]

In his footnote No. 85 in the above text Gilkerson continues on to quote from Norman Flayderman's correspondence with him. Flayderman adds:

"The gun was originally acquired in Europe and brought [to the United States] in the late 1940's. The relatively crude work on the inlay of the motto on the barrel contrasted with the rather sophisticated decoration elsewhere leads me to speculate that the barrel may be earlier than the later mechanism and decoration.., or possibly the barrel and the stock, with the mechanism and elaborate decoration later. I am most hesitant to venture theories without deeper research. The only thread of a clue that I have came from the late Harold Peterson many years ago when he saw the gun. He was going to undertake research on it, but sadly his untimely death prevented the project from ever getting off the ground. He did, however, mention the fact that he had seen a rather crude, large swivel gun, similar in nature, but much plainer and much less elaborate, in a Scottish museum that had a near identical inlaid motto on the barrel. Only recently have I tried to trace that one down... but with no results as yet."[160,161]

---

159  Ibid., page 99.
160  Ibid., page
161  This author followed in Flayderman's footsteps and spent many years also attempting to track down Harold Peterson's reference -- and has researched all of his files, now in the custody of the National Park Service of the Department of the Interior in Harpers Ferry, VA. After much work his file titled "Notes To Columbus Gun" was found in Series 11, Box 9. When opened the file was empty, except for a single hand-drawn sketch of a short barreled verso swivel gun – obviously not even close. All of Peterson's European Travel files from 1956 to 1973 were searched to produce a list of Scottish (and all UK) museums he visited. Then correspondence was exchanged between this author and these museums about this elusive specimen – all to no avail.

So, in sum, Gilkerson and Flayderman's conclusions about the gun were basically that:

1. It is probably the world's oldest known espingole.

2. It was difficult to date with precision.

3. Had an extremely early style of stock.

4. Relic beckoned further scholarship.

5. Columbus motto on barrel was enigmatic.

6. Barrel inscription more primitive than gun's other embellishments.

7. Pending further research, all is speculative regarding the story of this extremely early espingole.

8. Speculates that stock and barrel might be earlier than lock mechanism and decor, but still hesitant to venture theories without further research.

This author's response to Gilkerson and Flayderman's conclusions are as follows:

1. It is probably the world's oldest known espingole.
   <u>Response</u>: Author agrees.

2. It was difficult to date with precision.
   <u>Response</u>: Author agrees it was not an easy task, but is confidant this work has accomplished that.

3. Had an extremely early style of stock.
   <u>Response</u>: Author agrees.

4. Relic beckoned further scholarship.
   <u>Response</u>: Author agrees, but is confidant this work has accomplished that task.

5. Columbus motto on barrel was enigmatic.
   <u>Response</u>: Author is confidant this work has resolved that enigma. Neither Wilkerson nor Flayderman had researched the motto in depth to discover its limited date range of The Spring of 1493 to his death in 1506. After his death it was changed from: "POR CASTILLA Y POR LEON NUEVO MUNDO HALLO COLON" to "A CASTILLA Y A LEON NUEVO MUNDO <u>DIO</u> COLON." As explained earlier in this work, it was "DIO COLON" that appears on his tombs, etc.

6. Barrel inscription is more primitive than gun's other embellishments.
   <u>Response</u>: Author agrees. This is likely because the monarchs had several different craftsmen working on the gun at once, hastily getting it ready for his Second Voyage, then only weeks away. However, another thing to notice is that the same primitive hand that did

the inscription of the motto also did all of the other silver inlay décor from one end of the barrel to the other. Obviously, a different silversmith created all of the silver and gold heraldic cartouches and lion heads.

7.   Pending further research, all is speculative regarding the story of this extremely early espingole.

Response: Author agrees, but is confidant this work has accomplished that task and filled the information gaps.

8.   Speculates that stock and barrel might be earlier than lock mechanism and decor, but still hesitant to venture theories without further research.

Response: Firstly, Gilkerson never saw the gun in person, only via the 3 photos of it that appear on his page 98. In the study of this particular gun, the devil is in the details. This author has responded to this by including many close-up photos of every part of the gun. In addition, this microscopic examination led to the discovery that Pomegranate leaf petaloid edge decoration was actually a unifying theme on every part of the gun: lock, stock & barrel. For example, there is a broad forend barrel band of wrought steel with petaloid decorations on the rear edge. This same petaloid edge decoration appears on the edges of the lock plate, as well as the side plate, trigger guard, barrel bands, decorative heraldic medallions, swivel yoke, and even the tip of the muzzle -- thus showing all parts of the gun to be congruent, original and contemporary with each other. This also goes to show that the gun was made and assembled all at one time, and not the amalgamation of an older arquebus with later-added decorations.

In addition to all of the above, neither Gilkerson nor Flayderman took note of the extremely unique and complicated Automatic-Opening Pan Cover lock mechanism on the gun. In direct conversations with Flayderman, from whom the author acquired the gun, Norm just felt that because of its sophistication, he thought that the lock might be post-Columbus by a decade or so, and that the gun might have belonged to one of Columbus's sons, who in turn might have gifted it to Charles V. However, this theory doesn't fit because Columbus' sons were suing the Spanish crown for decades over being cut off from the 10% of New World revenues promised by Ferdinand and Isabella in the 1492 *Capitulation*, but which had since been withheld. Moreover, as shown earlier in the text, the heraldic décor on the gun is not that of Charles V, but that of Ferdinand and Isabella dated to 1492 by its pomegranate at the bottom of their royal crest silver medallion.

Also, neither Gilkerson nor Flayderman could be reasonably blamed for not knowing about the 1491-2 lost Madrid Codexes which shows Da Vinci's drawing of the Automatic-Opening Pan Cover lock mechanism on the gun. Although the Codexes had been discovered by the 1993 publication date of BOARDERS AWAY II, it took several decades for the Codexes to be transcribed, translated and published. Even then it took decades more for the information in them to be absorbed into the many specialized areas of the academic world. Even when the United Nations announced their finding in Anna Maria Brizio's 1974 article in the UNESCO Courier – no mention of the Matchlock was made!

## OVERALL CONCLUSION REGARDING OTHER LEONARDO "FINGERPRINTS" ON THE COLUMBUS GUN AND THE GUN ITSELF:

As stated in the Introduction, it is impossible to know after 500+ years exactly and precisely how much of the Columbus Gun (beyond the lock) can be attributed to Da Vinci, either directly, indirectly or through his students/apprentices.

However, it does seem like an improbable coincidence that the one and only known gun with his identifiably unique matchlock ignition mechanism is also adorned with his distinctive Dragons and other sophisticated artistic images and allegorical scenes that also appear in other Da Vinci works of art.

What do all these other "fingerprints" and associations mean? Did Leonardo contribute more than just the lock mechanism for this gun?

The author has made assertions in this work that he believes there are no other reasonable explanations for. These principal assertions have been:

— Gun was made circa 1493.

— Queen Isabella was presenter of the gun.

— Christopher Columbus was the recipient of the gun.

— Da Vinci invented the gun's lock mechanism.

— Da Vinci made (directly or indirectly) additional contributions to the gun's design and/or decoration.

Each reader will have to use their own standard of proof in weighing all this evidence. What should that standard be:

— More likely than not.

— The preponderance of the evidence.

— Clear and convincing evidence.

— Beyond a reasonable doubt.

As the saying goes: "We report --- you decide."

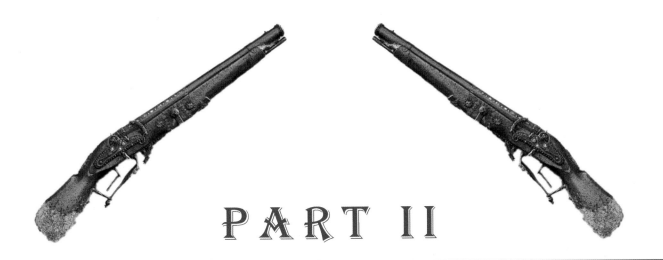

# PART II

# GUNS OF COLUMBUS
## - ALL TYPES -

# GUNS OF COLUMBUS - ALL TYPES[162]

D id Columbus Have Guns?

Yes – Lots of Them:

1. Signal Gun – Mortar

2. Handgonne – Hand Cannon or Pistole

3. Verso – Swivel Cannon

4. Bombard-Lombard

5. Arquebus – Serpentine Matchlock

6. Espingole – Swivel Arquebus (Columbus-Da Vinci Gun)[163]

The Great Explorer has been generally depicted in history as a venturesome sailor with a compass, an astrolabe and a dream. But the man with a dream was also a man with a gun. In fact, lots of them! This Part II of the book will be the first comprehensive explanation of the guns and cannons used on his 4 voyages, battles with the Taino Indians, etc.

As M. L. Brown records in his ground-breaking and highly-recommended book, <u>Firearms in Colonial America</u>, Chapter II's section on "Firearms of the Columbian Expeditions":

"Among the limited inventory of defensive and offensive weapons aboard the Nina, Pinta and Santa Maria sailing from Palos harbor with the early morning tide of August 3, 1492 were the

---

162 The War Museum's COLUMBUS GUN COLLECTION LIST: 1.Two Signal Mortars – Type Used On All Voyages; 2. A Handgonne – Type Used On All Voyages; 3. A Columbus Verso From His 4th Voyage; 4. A Bombard-Lombard – Type Used On All Voyages; 5. Serpentine Arquebus – Type Used On All Voyages; 6. The Da Vinci-Designed Espingole – 2nd Voyage. Unless stated otherwise, all guns shown in this Part II are in the War Museum's COLUMBUS GUN COLLECTION.
163 As discussed and illustrated in Part I above.

ships' cannon, a few crossbows, a Turkish bow, and one hand cannon; vestige of a vanishing age. (1)"[164]

M. L. Brown's footnote for this list cites Harold L. Peterson's Pageant of the Gun, but Peterson provides no citation for the list. This author has reviewed Peterson's archives at the Nation Park Service, but his own "Columbus file" there has no source or reference to it either. However, Peterson refers to the list as pertaining to "weapons of the landing party," not Columbus' entire fleet.[165] Thus, the question as to exactly how many guns in total, (and of what types) were on that First Voyage seems destined to remain unresolved.

May 1493 - a New fleet Equipped for his Second Voyage with Guns:

"A royal order had put all ships and appurtenances in the ports of Andalusia at the demand of Fonseca and Columbus . . . . . everything was hurriedly gathered for the armament, for it was of the utmost importance that the preparations should move faster than the watching diplomacy.

"Artillery which had been in use on shipboard for more than a century and a half was speedily amassed. The arquebuse, however, had not altogether been supplanted by the matchlock, and was yet preferred in some hands for its lightness. Military stores which had been left over from the Moorish war and were now housed in the Alhambra, at this time converted into an arsenal, were opportunely drawn upon."[166]

The National Rifle Association (NRA) also agrees that Christopher Columbus was the First to use Guns In The New World:

"The 15th century sailors under the command of Christopher Columbus — whose voyages nibbled at the edges of what became the United States — carried guns, says Jim Supica, Director of the NRA's National Firearms Museum in Virginia.

When one of the shipwrecks associated with Columbus and his colonization-discovery of Hispaniola was discovered a while back, matchlocks and a hand cannon were recovered from the wreckage. . . . .Underwater archaeologist Donald Keith says that guns of some type "were always present on every European voyage of discovery to the New World."[167]

---

164   M. L. Brown, Firearms in Colonial America – The Impact on History and Technology, 1492 - 1792, Washington, D.C., 1980, page 35.

165   Harold L. Peterson's Pageant of the Gun, New York, 1967, page 12.

166   JUSTIN WINSOR, CHRISTOPHER COLUMBUS AND HOW HE RECEIVED AND IMPARTED THE SPIRIT OF DISCOVERY, BOSTON AND NEW YORK, HOUGHTON, MIFFLIN AND COMPANY, The Riverside Press, Cambridge, 1891, [The Project Gutenberg Ebook # 42059 of Christopher Columbus and How He Received and Imparted the Spirit of Discovery by Justin Winsor], Page 258. These same facts are also separately confirmed in another section of this book sub-titles: "DOCUMENTATION OF USE."

167   Courtesy of CartersCountryGunsandAmmo · Gun Store, October 12, 2015. See also: http://www.nramuseum.com/guns/the-galleries/ancient-firearms-1350-to-1700.aspx

# THE SHIPS OF COLUMBUS - FLOATING FORTRESSES -

<u>SHIPS GUNS on the</u> *NINA and SANTA MARIA*:

T he traditional view that Columbus's ships of the first voyage were not heavily armed has been proven false in more recent times. The Catholic Kings constantly regarded Portugal as an omnipresent threat and there were known to be Portuguese spies in the Royal Court. As reported by Robert Fuson:

"The Nina (nee Santa Clara) was about the same size as the Pinta, according to the recent research of Eugene Lyon. She carried some 58—60 tons of cargo, was 67 feet long, had a beam of 21 feet, and a draft of just under 7 feet. An earlier computation by Martinez- Hidalgo, with whom Lyon consulted, made Nina out to be 70 feet in length, 23 feet in beam, and 5.8 feet in draft. The more recent, and slightly reduced, figures cited by Lyon are based on a detailed study of cargo and fittings. Though the smallest of the three vessels, Nina carried four masts. Originally lateen-rigged, she was square-rigged by Columbus during his stopover in the Canary Islands on the First Voyage. While researching the Libro de Armadas in the Archivo Generale de Indias in Seville, Lyon discovered, much to his surprise, that <u>Nina carried 10 breech-loading swivel guns. . . .</u>"[168]

168    LOG OF CHRISTOPHER COLUMBUS, Translated By Robert H. Fuson. International Marine Publishing, Camden, Maine, page 40.

## Placement of Versos aboard the Columbus Ships:
## Nina - Floating Fortress

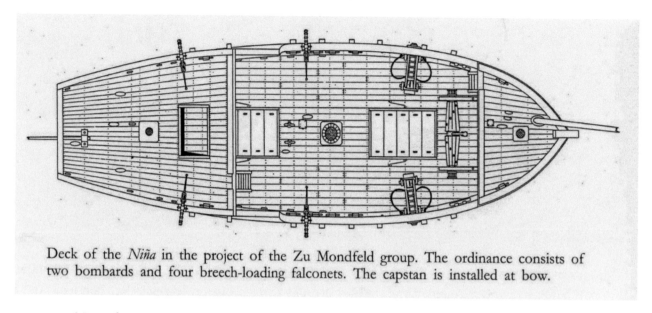

Deck of the *Niña* in the project of the Zu Mondfeld group. The ordinance consists of two bombards and four breech-loading falconets. The capstan is installed at bow.

Note the usual mix-up of nomenclature – bombarda vs. verso vs. falconet, etc.

# Santa Maria – Floating Fortress

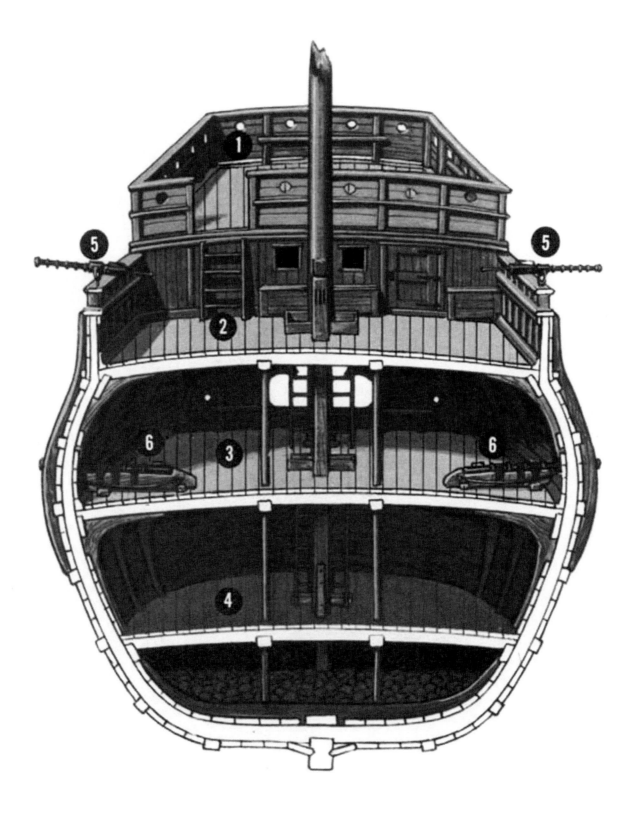

#5 = Versos on Main Deck. #6 = Bombards on Gun Deck.

**The SANTA MARIA, as shown in a woodcut in the printed version of The Letter of Columbus to the Catholic Kings, written in February 1493 during his return from the first voyage. Note all the gun ports on the starboard side and after deck.[169]**

169    Image courtesy of Cecil Jane, "The Journal of Columbus," New York 1960, page 193.

# 1. SIGNAL MORTARS – TYPE USED ON 1ˢᵀ AND ALL FOUR VOYAGES

Signal mortars were generally used for signaling the time of day (usually noon), and on Columbus' voyages to call the ships to rendezvous for a meeting of the Captains. It was prearranged during the first voyage that the first ship to sight land in the New World would fire one to notify the others. While some have speculated that they fired a regular cannon, this writer thinks that doing so would have been a waste of precious gunpowder and that the small signal mortar was all that was necessary, especially because sound travels well across water.

THE LOG OF CHRISTOPHER COLUMBUS: THE DISCOVERY OF NUEVA MUNDO - October 12, 1492:

> *"Shortly after midnight on October 12, 1492, Rodrigio de Triana, the lookout on the PINTA, spotted land in the distance. PINTA fired signal cannon to alert the other two ships that land had been sighted – making this the first gunfire heard in the New World."*[170]

## Two examples of signal mortars of the Age of Exploration.

---

170    LOG OF CHRISTOPHER COLUMBUS, Translated By Robert H. Fuson. International Marine Publishing, Camden, Maine.

## 2. HANDGONNE – TYPE USED ON ALL FOUR VOYAGES:

As noted above, Columbus carried handgonnes on the first and probably other voyages as well. This example is similar to one in the Real Armeria in Madrid, Spain at the bottom of a large showcase.

**Closeup**

**Overall view of the showcase**

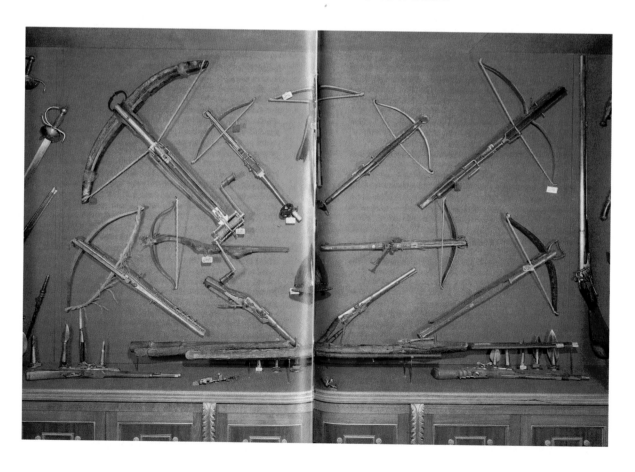

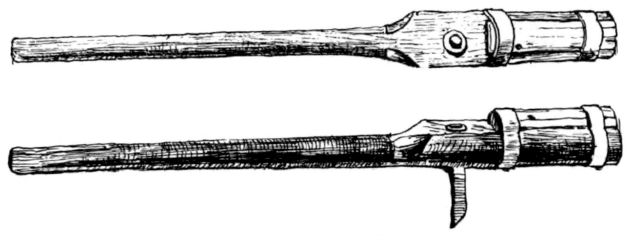

FIG. 14.—Harquebus at Berne.

*Dating from the late fourteenth or early fifteenth century, this four-barrelled hand gun weighs just over 4 lb.*
*Each barrel has a calibre of only 0·394 ins, is $3\frac{3}{8}$ ins long, and has its own touch-hole*

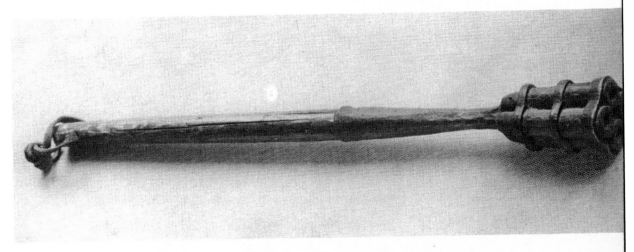

*One of the earliest hand guns in existence still mounted on its original tiller. The complete gun, just over*
*7 ins long, weighs more than 14 lb, and its calibre is $1\frac{3}{8}$ ins*

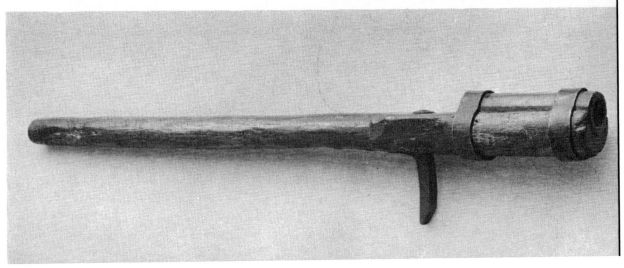

## 3. AN ACTUAL COLUMBUS VERSO FROM HIS 4<sup>TH</sup> VOYAGE - TYPE USED ON ALL FOUR VOYAGES

On May 11, 1502, Columbus began his Fourth Voyage when he put to sea from the port of Cadiz. with four old ships and 140 men under his command. Among those in the fleet were Columbus's brother Bartholomew, and his younger son Fernando, then just thirteen years old. At the age of fifty-one, Columbus was old, sick, and not welcome in his old home port of Santo Domingo. But the Admiral felt he had one more voyage left in him.

The nominal purpose of the trip was to find a strait linking the Indies (which Columbus still thought to be part of Asia) with the Indian Ocean. This strait was known to exist, since Marco Polo had traversed it on his way back from China. In effect, Columbus was looking for the Strait of Malacca (which is really near Singapore) in Central America, half a world away.

As he entered Caribbean waters, Columbus predicted that a hurricane was coming. He arrived at Santo Domingo on June 29, 1502, and requested that he be allowed to enter the harbor to shelter from the coming storm. He also advised the treasure fleet assembling in the harbor to stay put until the storm had passed. His request was treated with contempt by Nicolas de Ovando, the governor of Hispaniola, who denied Columbus entry to the port and sent the treasure fleet on its way.[171]

After he was refused anchorage in the harbor at Santo Domingo, Columbus took his ships west to the Hania River. To lighten the ships and get farther upriver to safety he ordered cannon and anchors thrown overboard. That is the place where this example below and 5 others were found in the 1960's by Charles " Bebe" Rebozo, a resident of Key Biscayne, Florida and friend of President Nixon. This probably happened in 1961 when Rebozo accompanied William Pawley (a CIA advisor-operative) on a secret mission to see Dominican Republic dictator Rafael Trujillo. Each cannon was found in rusted "relic" condition and each were about seven feet in length and weigh about 175+ pounds.

The Verso cannons were brought back to his Key Biscayne estate by Rebozo where they decorated the garden. However, after he died, his widow sent them to a junk yard. A Miami antique shop rescued them from the junk yard and sold them over a period of ten years. A small article about them appeared in an old cannon collectors' magazine in the 1970s. Upon learning about them it took the author, and current owner, 5 years to locate one of them and acquire it. A similar Columbus Verso is on display at the Columbus Lighthouse Museum in Santo Domingo, Dominican Republic.

---

171    When the hurricane hit, the treasure fleet was caught at sea, and twenty ships were sunk. Nine others limped back into Santo Domingo, and only one made it safely to Spain. Columbus's four ships all survived the storm with moderate damage. See webpage: http://www.columbusnavigation.com/v4.shtml

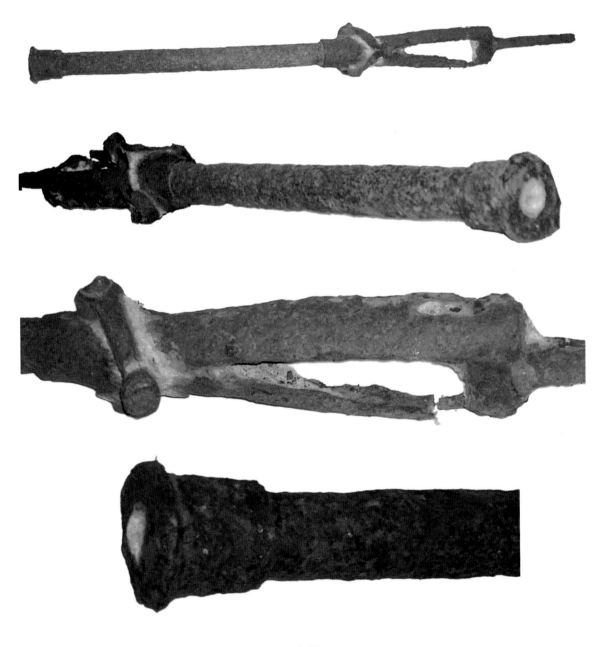

COLUMBUS VERSO
From 4th Voyage
Found by Bebe Rabozo
Archeological Dig Up The Hania
River West of Santo Domingo

**One of the Most Important Shipwrecks from the Age of Discovery is the Molasses Reef Wreck whose Excavated Armaments are on view at the Turks – Caicos Museum:**

**Armaments from the Molasses Reef Wreck: A Verso is on the upper right under the top of the Anchor (with half of barrel broken off). A Bombard is at the bottom of the photo on a reproduction sled base.**

The primary exhibit is centered on the Molasses Reef Wreck, the oldest European shipwreck excavated in the western hemisphere. This very early 1500s caravel (likely built in either Spain or Portugal) wrecked on the barrier reef edging the Caicos Banks south of Providenciales. Located at the museum is the Molasses Reef Wreck, which is dated to 1505 and is considered to be the oldest shipwreck located in the Americas.

A large number of arms, including cannons and small arms, bowls and storage jars, surgical and carpentry tools, as well as wooden pieces of the hull and metal pieces from the rigging, have been recovered from the wreck. Arms on the ship included two bombardettas, fifteen versos (a type of breech-loading swivel gun), haquebuts, haquebuzes (a smaller type of arquebus), grenades, crossbows and quarrels, swords, daggers, breech chambers (powder cartridges) for the bombardettas and versos, shot molds and sheets of Lead to be melted as needed to make a shot.[172]

---

172   Simmons, Joe J., III, Institute of nautical Archeology, Wrought-Iron ordnance: revealing discoveries from the New World, International Journal of Nautical Archeology and Underwater Exploration, 1988, 17.1. page 25. Underlining - emphasis by author.

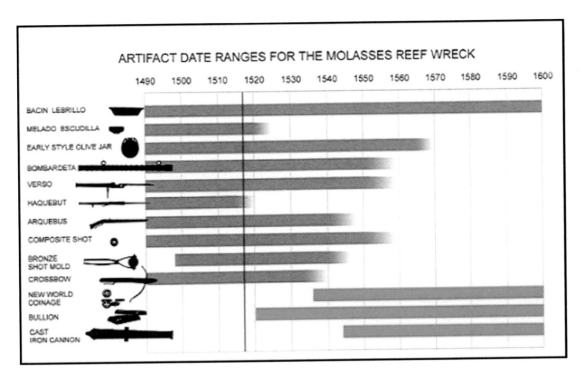

## ARTIFACT DATE RANGES FOR THE MOLASSES REEF WRECK

**BEER MUG BREECHLOADERS on Ferdinand Magellan's ship – Woodcut C.1589**[173]

FERDINANDES MAGALANES LVSITANVS anfractuoso euripo superato, Roo telluri ad Austrum nomen dedit, eiusque navis omnium prima atque novissima Solis cursum in terris æmulata, terra totus globum circumijt. An. Sal. ꝏ. D.XXII.

---

173   On image: 'FERDINAN. MAGALA.' In margin: 'FERDINANDES MAGALANES LVSITANVS...globum circumijt. An. Sal. ? .D.XXII', '4'. Americae Retectio (The Discovery of America), is a series of four plates (a picture atlas) commemorating the sucessive discoveries of America by Christopher Columbus, Americus Vespucci and Ferdinand Magellan.

**Early examples of breech loading artillery from the 15th to the 16th century on display at the Army Museum in Stockholm. The Verso-type breech-loading swivel guns are at the top, while the Lombard-Bombard is at the bottom. A translation of the main caption is as follows:**

"BREECH LOADERS FROM THE EARLY HISTORY OF ARTILLERY

"Until the middle of the 19th century almost all cannons were loaded from the front, but during the 15th and 16th century, breech loaders were fairly common. Most were made of welded iron bars fitted with reinforcing iron rings that have been shrunk around the bore, though breech loaders cast in iron or bronze were also produced. A name [in Swedish] for breech loading cannons were "föglare", a Swedish rendition of the German term "Vögler".

*Gunpowder chamber Wedge:*

"In the back of the bore a gun powder chamber was wedged shut. After the cannon had been fired, the wedge was knocked loose [by the crew], the chamber was removed, a new one inserted and wedged shut. With several prepared chambers, the fire rate could be quite high. However, the seal between the chamber and the bore was not good and the cannons could not withstand powerful charges."

## 4. A BOMBARD-LOMBARD – TYPE USED ON ALL VOYAGES

As can be seen by the armaments from the Molasses Reef Wreck, the Bombard, or Lombard, as they are interchangeably known, were the ships' "heavy artillery." They could be either breech-loading or muzzle-loading. If the former, the breech was simply a section of the barrel that was at the rear, and wedged together with the main longer end of the barrel. They did not have a separate "beer mug" shaped piece that dropped into a half-open section of the barrel. The placement of the Lombards aboard Columbus' ships can also be seen in the cutaway diagrams of the Nina and the Santa Maria, as shown in "Ships of Columbus" above.

There is ample documentation of their use in the "Log of Columbus" quoted extensively below.

**A rare antique 19th C. lithograph printed by the Real Armeria in Madrid shows this excellent example of a Lombard/Bombard.**

M. Pujadas, lit.                                                                                                  Montaner y Simon, Edit.

ARMAS DE LOS SIGLOS XIII Y XIV.

SIGLO XIII -1-Lanza -2-Espada de Fernando III el Santo-3-Alabarda ·
SIGLO XIV - 4 y 5 -Espadas-6-Partesana que perteneció à D. Pedro I el Cruel-7-Lombarda montada en su afuste
Las Armas de los nº 2 y 6 se conservan en la Armeria real de Madrid; las restantes en el Museo de Artilleria

**The photos below show an excellent example of a Columbus-era Lombard/Bombard mounted on a on a reproduction wooden sled base.**

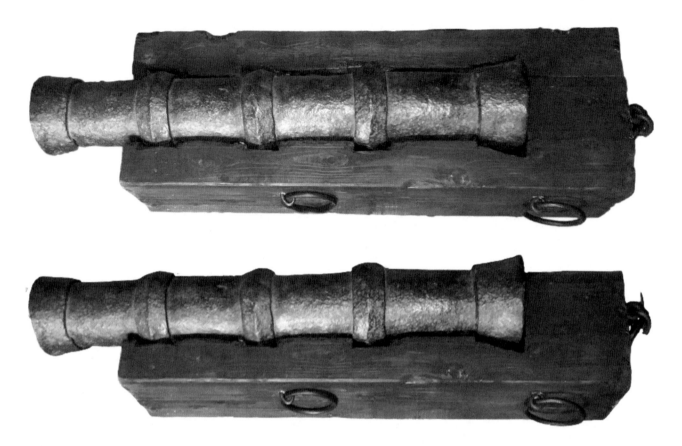

**AFTER THE SANTA MARIA RUNS AGROUND - SHOWING OFF THE GUNS:**

During the evening of Christmas Day, 25 December, 1492 the SANTA MARIA ran aground on a sand bar in a harbor on what is now the north coast of Haiti. Efforts to float the ship were to no avail and it became obvious the two remaining ships were not large enough to carry everybody back to Spain. However, volunteers to stay behind and collect gold from the natives were not lacking. Meanwhile, everything on the SANTA MARIA and eventually the ships timbers themselves needed to be moved ashore so that those remaining could build a fort out of her remains. Fortunately, the local Tainos were friendly and did the heavy lifting to help out. They also fed and housed Columbus's men generously.

**THE LOG OF CHRISTOPHER COLUMBUS - THE DISCOVERY OF ESPANOLA, (6 December 1492 to 15 January 1493) - Wednesday, 26 December 1492:**[174]

"The King dined with me on the Nina and afterwards went ashore with me, where he paid me great honor. Later we had a meal with two or three kinds of ajes, served with shrimp, game,

---

174   THE LOG OF CHRISTOPHER COLUMBUS, page 154.

and other foods they have, including their bread; which they call *cazabe*. Then the King took me to see some groves of trees near the houses, and fully 1,000 people, all naked, went with us. . . . Later, after we had eaten, the Indians took me to the beach, and I sent for a Turkish bow and a handful of arrows. I had a man from my company who was a skilled archer shoot the arrows. Inasmuch as the King did not know what arms are, since his people neither possess nor use them, the demonstration impressed him very much. . . . ."

"Nowhere in these lands is there knowledge of iron or steel, nor of any other metal except gold and copper, and I have seen very little of the latter."

"<u>I ordered that a lombard and a musket be fired, and the King was spellbound when he saw the effect of their force and what they penetrated. When the people heard the shots, they fell to their knees.</u>"[175]

*"I ordered that a lombard and a musket be fired, and the king was spellbound when he saw the effect of their force."*

---

175    Illustration credit: <u>THE LOG OF CHRISTOPHER COLUMBUS</u>, page 156. Emphasis (underlining) added. Note that a "musket" [harquebus], to be discussed in the next section, was also fired.

**THE LOG OF CHRISTOPHER COLUMBUS - THE DISCOVERY OF ESPANOLA, (6 December 1492 to 15 January 1493) - Wednesday, 2 January 1493.**

## A WEEK LATER COLUMBUS FIRES A LOMBARD AT THE *SANTA MARIA*:[176]

"I went ashore this morning to take leave of King Guacanagari and to depart in the name of the Lord. I gave the King one of my shirts and showed him the force of the lombards and their effect. For this purpose I ordered one loaded and fired at the side of the Santa Maria, which was aground. This all came about as a result of a conversation about the Caribes, with whom they were at war. The King saw how far the lombard shot reached and how it passed through the side of the ship. I also had the people from the ship fight a mock battle with their arms, telling the Cacique not to fear the Caribes if they came. I did all this so that the King would consider those I am leaving as friends, and also that he might fear them.

"I left on this Isla Espanola, which the Indians call Bohio, 39 men in the fortress, under the command of three officers..........

I have left with them all the merchandise which the Sovereigns had ordered purchased for trading, of which there is a large quantity. With this they may trade and barter for gold, together with everything the grounded ship carried. I also left them sufficient biscuits for a year and wine and much artillery. I also left the ship's boat, since most of them are sailors, so they can go find the gold mine when they see that the time is favorable. In this manner, when I return, I might find a lot of gold waiting and a place to establish a settlement, for this harbor is not to my liking. Since the gold that is brought here comes from the east, the more they went to the east the closer to Spain they would be. I also left seeds for sowing, and I left my officers, including the secretary and the master-at-arms, and among the others a ship's carpenter, a caulker, a good gunner who knows a great deal about machines, a caskmaker, a physician, and a tailor. All these men are also seamen.

**THE LOG OF CHRISTOPHER COLUMBUS - THE DISCOVERY OF ESPANOLA, (6 December 1492 to 15 January 1493) - Tuesday, 15 January 1493. [On the North coast of Samana Bay].[177]**

NATIVE WEAPONS:

"The bows of these people are as large as those in France and England. The arrows are just like the spears of the other people I have seen before, made from cane stalks that have gone to seed. They are very straight and one-and-a-half or two yards long, and they place a sharpened stick in the end, a palm-and-a-half long. At the end of this little stick some of them insert a fish tooth, and most of them put poison on the tip. They do not shoot as in other places, but in a peculiar way that cannot do much harm. The bows seem to be made of yew."

---

176   Ibid., page 161.
177   Ibid., page 175.

## 5. SERPENTINE ARQUEBUS – TYPE USED ON ALL VOYAGES

There are no examples of serpentine matchlock arquebusses known to the author that can be specifically documented to Columbus' four voyages, either from wreck sites or museums. Indeed surviving specimens of these guns from the Age of Exploration are few and far between. When they do surface on the collectors' market they generally go unrecognized and under-appreciated.

SCARCITY OF EARLY SPANISH FIREARMS IN GENERAL:

The Spanish Civil War (1936-39) caused the disappearance of a great number of antique firearms. At that time, under the Republic, possession of any firearm was an offence punishable by death. Consequently, owners of many fine and rare pieces destroyed them. This accounts for the paucity of Spanish firearms now in Spain outside a handful of public collections.

**A rare example below of a very Late 15th, or Early 16th Century, Spanish Serpentine Matchlock Found in Florida. Still in use after 300 years, the barrel was cut down and then rounded at the muzzle to take a Socket Bayonet in the 18th Century!**

Another rare example below of a very Late 15th, or Early
16th Century, Spanish Serpentine Matchlock. Fortunately,
the barrel was not cut down on this gun.

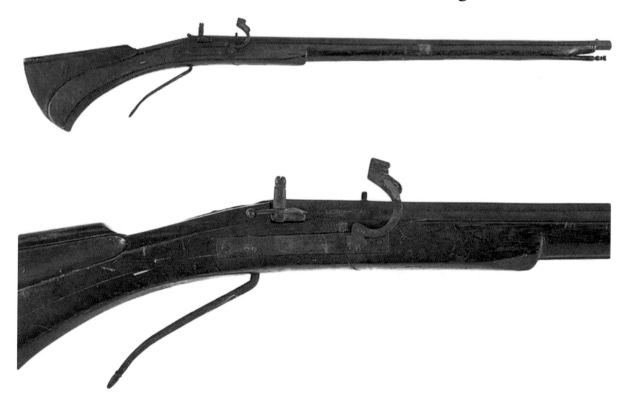

## THE BATTLE OF SANTO CERRO (HOLY HILL): THE FIRST MAJOR BATTLE IN THE NEW WORLD BETWEEN EUROPEANS VS. NATIVE AMERICANS, MARCH 14 -24, 1495: USE OF ARQUEBUSSES.

— Admiral/Governor/Viceroy Christopher Columbus and 200 armored Spanish infantrymen, including 100 Arquebussiers - Musketeers, 20 armored Spanish horsemen, fighting dogs and an uncounted thousands of Taíno allies (Cacique Guacanagarí's men) – against -

— 30,000 to 100,000 Taínos, the combined forces of Cacique Manicaotex and Cacique Guarionex's men.

— After 10 days – Columbus and his men could not gain any headway against the "primitive" Taíno warriors, who bore only stone war axes, and wooden clubs and spears.

This major grand-scale battle came during Columbus' 2nd Voyage. With its 17 Ships and 1500 Men, it has often been described as a Voyage of Conquest. Probably the best account of the battle, which also includes the most references to the weapons used on both sides was written by Professor Lynne A. Guitar (Ph.D. in Colonial Latin American History from Vanderbilt University). Her description is as follows:[178]

"On March 14, 1495, Admiral/Governor/Viceroy Christopher Columbus and 200 armored Spanish infantrymen, 20 armored Spanish horsemen, and an uncounted number of Taínos--Cacique Guacanagarí's men[179]--arrived at the site known as Santo Cerro ("Holy Hill"), a little to the northwest of today's town of La Vega in the Dominican Republic. They had left the settlement of La Isabela on the north coast and marched through the Pass of the Hidalgos en route to the main cacicazgo of Guarionex, in the heart of the mountainous, gold-bearing Cibao.[180] Just how long the march took is not mentioned in any of the surviving records. The Indians in the group probably outnumbered their Spanish allies by at least three to one, but the same thing happened at Santo Cerro as happened with battles later on in American history--the Europeans took all the credit in the stories that they told about the battle that ensued, minimizing the parts played by their Indian allies or leaving them entirely out of the official accounts.

---

178   Dr. Lynne A. Guitar, "WHAT *REALLY* HAPPENED AT SANTO CERRO? The First Major European/Indian Battle in the Americas; Origin of the Legend of the Virgin de las Mercedes, the Island's Patroness; and the Founding of Concepción de la Vega." An unpublished monograph, circa 2005, Santiago de Caballeros, Dominican Republic. Lynne A. Guitar (Ph.D. in Colonial Latin American History from Vanderbilt University), is a bilingual historian, cultural anthropologist, and specialist in the history and culture of the Taíno, the Natives of the Greater Antilles. She lived, worked, and researched in the Dominican Republic for 19 years, has starred in documentaries for the BBC, History Channel, and Discovery Channel, among others, and has published numerous professional articles and book chapters.
179   *Cacique* is the Taíno word for "chief" and his *cacicazgo* was the geographical region within which he was the political leader. Guacanagarí was the cacique of the region where Columbus's flagship, the *Santa María*, wrecked aboard a reef on Christmas Eve 1492. Gucanagarí was the Europeans' first Native American ally.
180   Columbus called the fertile valley La Vega Real, which translates literally as "The Royal Lowlands," but it continued to be called locally by its native name, Cibao ("Stoney Place"), and still is today.

The goal of the army of Spanish and Taíno warriors led by Columbus was to stamp out the increasing Indian attacks against the Spaniards (protests against Columbus' orders that each adult Taíno must pay an annual tribute of gold) and to establish a firm foothold in the gold-bearing region where, until now, they had only one small fort, Santo Tomás on the Jánico River—the name Santo Tomás, named for the Bible's "Doubting Thomas," was a riposte to those who had publicly expressed their doubt that Columbus would find much gold on Hispaniola. The Taíno cacique who had given them the most trouble to date, Caonabó (who was blamed for the massacre of the 39 Spaniards whom Columbus left behind at Fort la Navidad on his first voyage) had been captured, put aboard a ship bound for judgment in Spain, and had died at sea. But the attacks did not stop. One of Caonabó's brothers, named Manicaotex, was now leading the attacks against the Spaniards out of the cacicazgo of the Cacique Guarionex, which was tributary to Caonabó's cacicazgo of Maguá.

## COLUMBUS at the BATTLE of SANTO CERRO Carrying a Matchlock Arquebus, with the Holy Hill in the background, as depicted in a 17th C. German Engraving[181]

---

181    Collection of the author.

The Spaniards chose the site of Santo Cerro because it provided a clear view of the Cibao Valley below and because it was relatively easy to defend. It is a high, steep mountain on the northern edge of the vast chain called the Cordillera Central. From atop Santo Cerro, one can see across the entire Cibao Valley (approximately 24 kms. wide at this point), all the way northeast to the narrow but high mountain passes of the Cordillera Septentrional that give way to the Atlantic Coast near today's towns of Puerto Plata and Sosua.

What a sight awaited Columbus and his men as they looked down upon the Cibao Valley in the early light of dawn on the first day of battle. Reports vary, and the numbers probably grew over time, as often happens with legendary battles, but <u>it is estimated that somewhere between 30,000 and 100,000 Taínos, the combined forces of Manicaotex and Guarionex, were gathered at the foot of Santo Cerro, ready to do battle with the Spaniards and Guacanagarí's men. Witnesses testified there were "Indians as far as the eye could see."</u>[182]

## View of the battlefield from SANTO CERRO (Holy Hill)[183]

The Spaniards descended to do battle and, despite their thousands of Indian allies, <u>their horses, arquebuses (ancient rifles), steel spears and swords, fighting dogs, and advanced battle strategies that had been polished throughout 800 years of fighting Moors back in Spain, they could</u>

---

182    Emphasis (underlining) added.
183    Photo by author.

not gain any headway against the "primitive" Taíno warriors, who bore only stone war axes, and wooden clubs and spears. Outnumbered and out fought, the Spaniards were beaten back and back, up the steep mountain. Sources vary about how many days the battle lasted. It appears to have been about ten days later (March 25, 1495), with most of their Indian allies either killed or scattered, that Columbus ordered his men into the *palenque*, a palisaded area on the highest part of the mountain that he had ordered the Indians to construct. There, Columbus had also ordered a cross to be made out of the wood of a local *nispero* tree,[184] where he and his men prayed for their lives that night, which all believed would be their last. Witnesses later testified that they dreaded the dawn and the deaths that they were certain awaited them in the next day's battle.

Certain defeat was avoided by a series of "miracles" that occurred during the night, or so eyewitnesses reported. In the early hours after nightfall, enemy Indians tried to burn down the Spaniards' cross, but they could only scorch it, despite all the dry firewood they piled around it. Unsuccessful in burning down the Christian symbol, they tried to pull the cross down, using thick vines of the *bejuco* plant, but couldn't pull it down. Frustrated, they tried to chop the cross down with their stone axes, but were also unsuccessful. Fray Juan Infante of the Order of Mercederians was Columbus's private confessor. He not only witnessed all of the above Indian attacks on the cross, but was witness to a far more miraculous event. At about 9:00 PM, he claims he saw a light descend and envelop the cross, while a lady dressed all in white, with a baby in her arms, appeared on the right arm of the cross. He declared that the Virgen de las Mercedes had come to save the day for the Spaniards—the "Virgin of Mercies" was well known in Spain as the protector of those who were imprisoned.

---

184   Nispero's botanical name is *medlar*; it is commonly called Japanese Persimmon in English.

# View of the battlefield from SANTO CERRO (Holy Hill)[185]

It certainly appeared that Fray Juan Infante was right. In the morning, when the weary, bloody, frightened Spanish troops got up, ready to descend the mountain to do battle to the death, there was no one there to fight! Columbus ordered his men to kneel and pray in thanks to the Virgen de las Mercedes for their miraculous victory and to build a small fortress at the foot of Santo Cerro, just one-half league from Cacique Guarionex's main population center.

. . . . As an anthropologist who specializes in the history and culture of the Taínos, however, I think I know how the above events can be explained from a less Euro-centric viewpoint. That battle in March of 1495, the very first major battle between Europeans and Indians, was a clash not only of warriors and weaponry, but of traditions and beliefs. The Taínos did not know that Spaniards fought to the death, or at least until one side officially surrendered and a treaty agreement was negotiated, spelling out the terms of both the conquest and the defeat. Conversely, the Spaniards did not know that Taínos fought (albeit rarely) until one side was clearly the winner. No written surrender or official treaty was needed among Indians. The gain

---

185  From an 17-18th Century engraving from Santo Domingo, Dominican Republic.

was clear for all to see, so the battle ended, and both sides went back home to continue the normal life cycle of planting, harvesting, fishing, hunting, and raising families.

At Santo Cerro in March of 1495, it appears that both the Taínos and the Spaniards thought they had won. The Taínos, knowing that they were clearly the victors, having killed or scattered the Spaniards' allies and beaten the European soldiers back and up the mountain as far as they could go, just went home the night the battle ended, as was their norm--the attacks on the cross may have been a final nose-flip at the losers. When the Spaniards awoke to an empty battlefield, however, they assumed that the Taínos had fled!"

## 16th C. MS Shows 1475 Battle with Serpentine Matchlock Arquebusses

## 1496 Drawing of the Fortress at Santo Domingo Shows Placement of Serpentine Arquebusses

**SERPENTINE ARQUEBUSSES at SDQ**

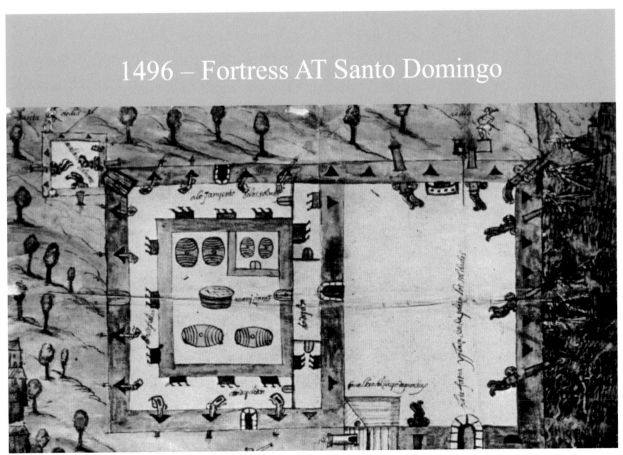

1496 – Fortress AT Santo Domingo

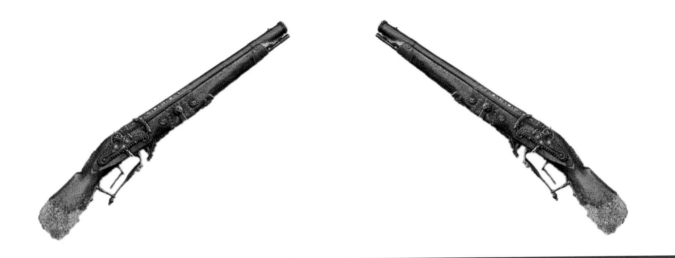

# ESTE ES EL FIN

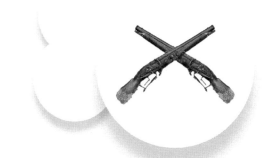

# APPENDIX A

## CHRONOLOGIES, DATES AND PEOPLE

### IMPORTANT DATES IN EARLY FIREARMS TECHNOLOGY

1247 – 1$^{st}$ Gunpowder at Siege of Seville

1281 – Turin orders hand cannons

1327 – Cannon used by Edward III

1364 – 1$^{st}$ Hand Cannon: Edward III

1375 – 1$^{st}$ Hand Gonnes in England

1424 – Mechanical device for firing

1474 – 1$^{st}$ Shooting Matches

1475 – Lever Trigger: Codex Germanicus 597

1492 – Da Vinci's Automatic-Opening Pan Cover Codex Madrid

1498 – Rifling invented

1500 – 1510 - 1$^{st}$ Wheel Locks in Leonardo da Vinci's Codex Atlanticus

1490 – 1530 – 1$^{st}$ Matchlock 10-shot Revolver (Germany)

1500 - 1506 – Wheelocks ("self-igniting" guns) banned from shooting matches

1510 – 1540's – Henry VIII has breech loading matchlock Arquebus

## THE FOUR VOYAGES OF CHRISTOPHER COLUMBUS

1st Voyage: 1492 – 1493

2nd Voyage: 1493 – 1496

3rd Voyage: 1498 – 1500

4th Voyage: 1502 – 1504

Death of Queen Isabella – November 26, 1504

Death of Columbus – May 20, 1506

Death of King Ferdinand – January 23, 1516


THE RULERS of SPAIN: 1400 - 1700

Although Muslim forces conquered much of the Iberian Peninsula during the eighth century, several Christian enclaves remained, composed of Visigoths and Franks. These groups developed into new kingdoms, and during the tenth century they began a process of re-conquest. As these kingdoms expanded, two came to dominate: Castile and Aragon. The early history of modern Spain is very much in the relationship between these two powers that were united - in theory at least – by the marriage in 1469 between Ferdinand of Aragon and Isabella of Castile & Leon. This "united" Spain lasted until the death of Isabella in 1505. Ferdinand became Regent for parts of Isabella's kingdom until his death in 1516 when Spain was again united under the Habsburg Dynasty.

This is a chronological list of the people who have ruled Spain; the dates given are the periods of said rule. The list begins with the respective rulers of Castile and Aragon, before moving on to those of the united Spain.


### Castile and León

1390 - 1406 Henry III

1406 - 1454 John II

1454 - 1474 Henry IV

1474 - 1504 Isabella

1504 - 1506 Joanna the Mad (Habsburg)

1506 Phillip I

1506 - 1516 Ferdinand II (of Aragon, as regent for Joanna the Mad)

## Aragon

**1395 - 1410 Martin I**

**1412 - 1416 Ferdinand**

**1416 - 1458 Alfonso V**

**1458 - 1479 John II**

**1479 - 1516 Ferdinand II**

## Unified 'Spain' Habsburg Dynasty

**1516 - 1556 Charles I (Emperor Carlos/Charles V)**

**1556 - 1598 Philip II**

**1598 - 1621 Philip III**

**1621 - 1665 Philip IV**

**1665 - 1700 Charles II**

## Bourbon Dynasty

**1700 - 1724 Philip V**

## CHRONOLOGY of the RECONQUISTA

**1461**
**'All Abü'l-Hassan' Alî becomes Amir of Granada.**

**1462**
**Granada loses Gibraltar and Archidona.**

**1462—72**
**Peasant revolt and civil war in Aragon; major rebellion against MarInid rulers of Morocco.**

**1469**
**Marriage of Princess Isabel of Castile and Prince Fernando of Aragon.**

**1471**
**Portuguese take Arzila and Tangier.**

**1472**

Muhammad al-Shaykh becomes first Wattasid ruler of central Morocco.

**1474**

Death of King Enrique IV of Castile; succeeded by Queen Isabel.

**1475**

Peasant revolt in Kingdom of Aragon.

**1478**

Truce between Castile and Granada.

**1479**

Death of King Juan II of Aragon; succeeded by Fernando II (1479—1516); Castile and Aragon united under the joint rule of Isabel and Fernando.

**1481 (Dec 26)**

Granadans seize Zahara.

**1482 (Feb 28)**

Castilians seize Aihama; (March—July) unsuccessful Moorish attempts to retake Alhama; (July 15) Abü'l Hassan defeats Fernando's attempt to take Loja; Abü'l-Hassan toppled by a palace coup in favour of his son Muhammad XII in Granada, who establishes rival capital in Malaga.

**1483**

Congress of leaders of the Castilian Hermandad to reform this organisation; (March—April) Castilians defeated in the mountains behind Malaga; (April 20) Muhammad XII captured during an unsuccessful raid against Lucena; released after making a treaty with Fernando and Isabel; Abü'l-Hassan regains Granada; (September 17) Granadan raid towards Cordoba defeated at Lopera; (October) Granadan legal authorities deny Muhammad XIi's right to the throne; Castilians retake Zahara.

**1484**

Spanish fleets sent to patrol Strait of Gibraltar; Genoa and Venice threatened with reprisals if they help Granada; large Castilian raid as far as the Mediterranean coast; (June) Fernando takes Alora and Setenil; (late summer) Castilian raid into the Vega of Granada.

**1461**

'Ali Abu l-Hassan 'Ali becomes Amir of Granada.

1462.

Granada loses Gibraltar and Archidona.

1462—72

Peasant revolt and civil war in Aragon; major rebellion against Marinid rulers of Morocco.

1469

Marriage of Princess Isabel of Castile and Prince Fernando of Aragon.

1471

Portuguese take Arzila and Tangier.

1472

Muhammad al-Shaykh becomes first Wattasici ruler of central Morocco.

1474

Death of King Enrique IV of Castile; succeeded by Queen Isabel.

1475

Peasant revolt in Kingdom of Aragon.

1478

Truce between Castile and Granada.

1479

Death of King Juan II of Aragon; succeeded by Fernando II (1479—1516); Castile and Aragon united under the joint rule of Isabel and Fernando.

1481 (Dec 26)

Granadans seize Zahara.

1482 (Feb 28)

Castilians seize Alhama; (March—July) unsuccessful Moorish attempts to retake Alhama; (July 15) Abü'l- Hassan defeats Fernando's attempt to take Loja; Abu l-Hassan toppled by a palace coup in favour of his son Muhammad XII in Granada~ who establishes rival capital in Malaga.

1483

Congress of leaders of the Castilian Hermandad to reform this organization; (March—April) Castilians defeated in the mountains behind Malaga; (April 20). Muhammad XII captured during an unsuccessful raid against Lucena; released after making a treaty with Fernando and Isabel; Abü'l-Hassan regains Granada; (September 17) Granadan raid towards Cordoba defeated at Lopera; (October). Granadan legal authorities deny Muhammad Xli's right to the throne; Castilians retake Zahara.

## 1484

Spanish fleets sent to patrol Strait of Gibraltar; Genoa and Venice threatened with reprisals if they help Granada; large Castilian raid as far as the Mediterranean coast; (June) Fernando takes Alora and Setenil; (late summer) Castilian raid into the Vega of Granada.

## 1485 (January)

Auto da Fé in Seville burns 19 men and women, making total of 500 conversos convicted as heretics; Abu l-Hassan incapacitated by a stroke and replaced by his brother Muhammad al-Zagal as Muhammad XIII; Watasid ruler of Fez makes a treaty of friendship with Spain; (spring) Castilians take Coin and Cartama, raid Malaga area, take Ronda and Marbella; Granadan raid into the area of Medina-Sidonia; unsuccessful Castilian attempt to take Moclin is diverted to take Cambil and Albahar; Muhammad XII returns to Granada with Castilian support; civil war in Granada between Muhammad XII 'Boabdil' and Muhammad XIII al-Zagal; (February) al-Zagal takes Almeria from Muhammad XII who flees to Castile.

## 1486

Reconciliation between Muhammad XII and Muhammad XIII; (June) Castilians take Loja and capture Muhammad XII, also take Illora and Moclin; Castilians raid Granada and defeat Muslim sortie at Pinos Puente, but then suffer serious losses outside Granada; another treaty signed between Muhammad XII, and Fernando and Isabel; (September 15) Muhammad XII regains city of Granada with Castilian help but al-Zagal retains the Aihambra;

## 1487 (April 27)

Fernando takes Vélez Malaga; Muhammad al-Zagal loses support in Granada and goes to Almeria; (May) third treaty signed by Muhammad XII 'Boabdil', Fernando and Isabel; (August) Castilians take Malaga.

## 1488

Early in the year Spanish forces help the Duke of Brittany against the Regent of France but are defeated; political difficulties within Castile and Aragon; Fernando invades the eastern Amirate of Granada, taking Vera, but is driven off by al-Zagal's garrisons; several counter-raids by al-Zagal's forces into Castile.

## 1489 (August)

Muhammad al-Shaykh, ruler of Fez, forces Portuguese to abandon the building of a fortress near Wadi Lukkus, then renews his peace treaty with Portugal; plagues and floods in Andalusian Castile; (December) Castilians take Cuxar and Baza; peace treaty between Muhammad XIII al-Zagal, Fernando and Isabel.

**1490**

Muhammad XII refuses to surrender Granada, authorizes counter-raids, retakes Aihendin (June 15), encourages revolt in Guadix, unsuccessfully attempts to take Salobreña and Adra; Castilians raid the Vega of Granada and crush rebellion in Guadix.

**1491 (April 26)**

Start of the final siege of Granada; (July) Castilian siege camp outside Granada is burned down and replaced by a permanent town named Santa Fe; (November 15) surrender agreement ratified by Granada and Spanish rulers.

**1492 (Night of Jan 1-2)**

Spanish troops enter the Alhambra; official surrender of Granada the following day; (January 6) Fernando and Isabel enter Granada.

# TERMINOLOGY: ARQUEBUS-HARQUEBUS-ESPINGARDA-ESPINGOLE

Confusion reigned supreme in early firearms terminology of the 15th through 17th centuries. As the noted author and authority, Claude Blair, stated:

"The term arquebus has had several different meanings during its period of use. Generally, however, it has meant a light portable firearm with a stock enabling it to be held against the cheek, chest or shoulder. In the beginning it was also distinguished from the hand cannon by having a serpentine to hold the lighted match by which it was fired."[186]

Victor Gay, in his Glossafre Archeologique (Vol.1, p.73), quotes a Latin document of 1417, concerning the term "arcubusarils" and another of 1475, in French, mentioning the terms "hacquebusies" and "arquebuse de fer." 'the term "l'archibusio" was referred to in the work, written in 1465, of an Italian, Francesco de Giorgio Martini (1423—1506), and quoted by Colonel Favé (Etudes sur le Passé et l'Avenir de l'Artillerle, Paris, 1862, Vol. 3).[187]

The first arquebuses were little different in appearance from the hand cannon, according to a text of 1478: "...paid to Perrinot Poinsard, for the price of three francs each, twelve arquebuses (liar quebuczes) , six with iron butts and the others with wooden butts." (cited by V. Gay, Glossaire 1, p. 73).

As time passed, the word arquebus came to have different meanings which varied according to the time and the nationality of the person using it. [The Spanish, for example often used the term: ESPINGARDA-ESPINGOLE][188]

---

186    Blair, Claude, European and American Arms, London, 1962.
187    Bosson, Clement, "Que salt-on de l'Haquebute?" in Annes Anciennes, Vol. 2, No. 1, Geneva, 1957.
188    Author's note.

After the musket became popular about the middle of the sixteenth century, the term arquebus, at least in English-speaking countries, was used to denote a lighter arm that could be fired without a rest. In other instances, it was used to indicate a wheel lock as opposed to a matchlock, but after 1550 it almost always referred to a light firearm, whether for military or sporting purposes. CLB."[189,190]

189  ENCYCLOPEDIA OF FIREARMS, Edited by HAROLD L. PETERSON, E.P. DUTTON AND COMPANY INC., New York 1964.
190  See also: Peterson, Harold L., Arms and Armor in Colonial America, 1526—1783, Harrisburg, Pa., 1956. Peterson, Harold L., The Treasury of the Gun, New York, 1962 (The Book of the Gun, London, 1963).

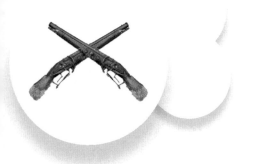

# APPENDIX C

# BIBLIOGRAPHY

Albaladejo. Pablo Fernandez. _"Cities and the State in Spain." In Cities and the Rise of States in Europe, A.D. 1100 to 1800._ edited by Charles Tilly and Wim P. Blockmans, 168-83. Boulder: Westview Press, 1994.

Alonso, Martinez de Espinar. _Arte de Ballesteria y Monteria_. Madrid, 1644.

Anonymous, _Catdlogo de los objetos de la Real Armeria_, Madrid, 1861.

Beazley, Charles Raymond, _Encyclopedia Britannica,_ Cambridge University Press., 741-746.

Benjamin, Keen, _"The life of the Admiral Christopher Columbus by his son Ferdinand,_ New Jersey, Rutgers, 1959.

Berend, Nora. _"Frontiers." In Palgrave Advances in the Crusades_, edited by Helen J. Nicholson. New York: Palgrave Macmillan. 2005.

Bergreen, Lawrence. _Columbus: The Four Voyages, 1493–1504_. Penguin Group US.

Bernal Diaz del Castillo, _Historia verdadera de la conquista de Nueva Espana_ , Mexico: Pedro Robredo, 1939.

Bonaventura, _Pistofilo, Oplomachia._ Siena, 1621.

Buttin, Charles. _'I/Arquebuserie de Ripoll.'_ Published in a series of articles in Armes a Feu et Armes Blanches, 1914.

Cecil Jane (ed. and trans.), _Select Documents Illustrating the Four Voyages of Columbus_ London: Hakluyt Society, 1930.

Cervantes Saavedra, *Miguel de, Segunda Parte del Ingenioso Caballero Don Quixote de la Mancha*. Madrid, 1615.

Clephan, Robert Coltman, *An Outline of the History and Development of Hand Firearms From the Earliest Period to About the End of the Fifteenth Century*. London, Walter Scott, 1906.

Cohen, J.M. *The Four Voyages of Christopher Columbus*:. London UK: Penguin Classics. 1969.

Columbus, Christophe, *Select Letters of Christopher Columbus: With Other Original Documents, Relating to His Four Voyages to the New World,* London,1847.

Columbus, Christopher, *Book of Prophecies,* Jerome Millon, 1992.

Columbus, Christophe, *The Journal of Christopher Columbus (During His First Voyage)*. Cambridge University Press.

Columbus, Christopher *First Voyage to America: From the log of the "Santa Maria"*. Dover. (1991) [1938].

Columbus, Christopher *Select Letters of Christopher Columbus: With Other Original Documents, Relating to His Four Voyages to the New World*. London: The Hakluyt Society. 1847.

Columbus, Christopher *Encyclopedia Britannica. 6 (11th ed.)*. Cambridge University Press. pp. 741–746. (1911).

Columbus, Christopher; Markham, Clements R. (ed.). The Journal of Christopher Columbus (During His First Voyage). Cambridge University Press. Toscanelli, Paolo (2010) [1893].

Columbus, Ferdinand *A History of the Life and Actions of Adm. Christopher Columbus*. in Churchill, Awnsham, 1732.

Conner, Jeanette Thurber, (ed. and trans)., *Colonial Records of Spanish Florida*. DeLand, The Florida State Historical Society, 1930.

Cook, Weston F. *"The Cannon Conquest of Nasrid Spain and the End of the Reconquista."* 43-70. Journal of Military History 57, 1993.

Cossio, Jose Maria, ed., *AiUobiografias de soldados*. (BAE 90). Madrid, Ediciones Atlas, 1956.

Covarrubias, Sebastian de. *Tesoro de la lengua castellana 0 espanola.* , 3 vols, Madrid, 1611. Diaz del

Castillo, Bernal, *Historia verdadera de la conqidsta de Nueva Espana*. Mexico, Pedro Robredo, 1939, 3 vols.

Crosby, A.W. *The Columbian Voyages: the Columbian Exchange, and their Historians*. Washington, DC: American Historical Association. 1987.

Davidson, Miles H. *Columbus then and now: a life reexamined*. Norman, OK: University of Oklahoma Press. 1997.

De Mariana. Juan. *"The Conquest of Granada (1601)." In Early Modern Spain*: A Documentary History, edited by Jon Cowans, 12-14. Philadelphia: University of Pennsylvania Press, 2003.

Del Pulgar. Hernando. *"Cronica de los reyes catolicos chapters 141 and 176."* In Documents on the Later Crusades, 1274-1580, edited by Norman Housley, New York: St. Martin's Press, 1996.

Dugard, Martin. *The Last Voyage of Columbus: Being the Epic Tale of the Great Captain's Fourth Expedition, Including Accounts of Swordfight, Mutiny, Shipwreck, Gold, War, Hurricane, and Discovery*. Little, Brown. (2005).

Dyson, John Columbus. *For Gold, God and Glory*. Madison Press Books. (1991). Edited by Norman

Housley, Norman. *Crusading in the Fifteenth Century*. New York: Palgrave Macmillan, 2004.

Edwards, John. *"Espana es Diferente'? Indulgences and the Spiritual Economy in Late Medieval Spain." In Promissory Notes on the Treasury of Merits*: Indulgences in Late Medieval Europe, edited by R.N. Swanson, 147-68. Leiden: Brill, 2006

Edwards, John. "Reconquista and Crusade in Fifteenth-Century Spain." In Crusading in the Edwards, John, Ferdinand and Isabella. London: Pearson Education Limited, 2005.

Estruch y Cumella, D. Jose. *Museo Armeria.* Barcelona, 1896.

Foronda y Aguilera, *Manuel de. Estancias y viajes del emperador Carlos V.* Madrid, 1914.

Froom, LeRoy *The Prophetic Faith of our Fathers* (Djvu and PDF). 1. (1950).

Fuson, Robert H. *The Log of Christopher Columbus.* International Marine Publishing (1992).

Garcia, Luis Ribot. *"Types of Armies: Early Modern Spain." In War and Competition Between States, edited by Philippe Contamine, 37-68*. New York: Oxford University Press, 2000.

Gayetano Rosell (ed.), *Cronicas de los reyes de Costilla* Madrid: Imprenta de los Sucesores de Hernando, 1919.

Gaztambide, Jose Goñi. "*The Holy See and Reconquest of Granada.*" In *Spain in the Fifteenth Century*, edited by Roger Highfield. London: The Macmillan Press Ltd, 1972.

Genova, J. *Armas de Caza.* Barcelona, 1901.

Guiance, Ariel. "*To die for country, land or faith in Castilian medieval thought.*" Journal of Medieval History 24 (1998).

Hackett, Charles Wilson, *Historical Documents Relating to New Mexico, Nueva Vizcaya, and Approaches Thereto, to 1773.* Washington, Carnegie Institution, 1923.

Hoff, Arne, „*Hjullaase med seglformet hanefjer.*" Vaabenhistoriske Aarboger, 1940.

Hoopes, Thomas T., „*Ripollsche Radschlosspistolen.*" Zeitschrift fur historische Waffenkund Kostiimkunde, Vol. IV.

Horwitz, Tony *A Voyage Long and Strange: Rediscovering the New World,* (1st ed.). New York: Henry Holt and Co. (2008).

Jane, Cecil, (ed. and trans.), *Select Documents Illustrating the Four Voyages of Columbus. London*, Hakluyt Society, 1930.

Joseph, Edward Lanzar. *History of Trinidad.* A.K. Newman & Co. (1838).

Jovellanos, Gaspar Melchor de, *Diarios. Julio Somoza, ed. Oviedo,* Institute de Estudios Asturianos, 1953.

Jubinal, Achille, *La Armeria Real ou Collection des Principales Pieces de la Galerie d³Armes Anciennes de Madrid,* 3 vols, Paris, 1845.

Laking, Guy Francis, *The Armoury of Windsor Castle.* London; Bradbury, Agnew, 1904.

Lavin, James D., "*An Examination of Some Early Documents Regarding the Use of Gunpowder in Spain.*" Journal of the Arms and Armour Society, IV, (March, 1964).

Lenk, Torsten. *Flintlaset dess uppkomst och utveckling.* Stockholm, 1939.

Lopez, Barry *The Rediscovery of North America.* Lexicon, KY: University Press of Kentucky. (1990).

Marchesi, Jose Maria, *Catdlogo de la Real Armeria.* Madrid, 1849.

Martin, Kluge, *The Wealthy Fuggers,* Regio Augsburg Tourismus.

Mateos, Juan. *Origen y Dignidad de la Caza.* Madrid, 1634.

Michel, Lévy Frères, Baron de Nervo : Isabelle la Catholique, editions, Col. Temple-West, 1897.

Morison, Samuel Eliot *Admiral of the Ocean Sea: A Life of Christopher Columbus.* Boston: Little, Brown and Company. (1942).

Murphy, Patrick J.; Coye, Ray W. *Mutiny and Its Bounty: Leadership Lessons from the Age of Discovery*. New Haven, CT: Yale University Press. (2013).

Neal, W. Keith, *Spanish Guns and Pistols*. London, G. Bell and Sons, 1955.

Nunez Alba, Diego, *Didlogos de Diego Nunez Alva de la vida del Soldado*. Salamanca, 1552.

Ostendi, Colonel Don Joachim Martinez. *Guia del Visatante Museo del Ejercito*. Madrid, 1954.

Petrini, Antonio, *Armeria universale de Antonio de Petrini. Manuscript*, Metropolitan Museum of Art, New York, n.d. (ca. 1640).

Phillips, Jr, William D.; Phillips, Carla Rahn. *The Worlds of Christopher Columbus*. Cambridge, UK: Cambridge University Press. (1992).

Pope Sixtus IV. *"Pope Sixtus IV grants the cruzada to Ferdinand and Isabella for the war against Granada, 10 August 1482."* In Documents on the Later Crusades, 1274-1580, edited by Norman Housley. 156-62. New York: St. Martin's Press. 1996.

Robert Goltman Clephan, *An Outline of the History and Development of Hand Firearms from the Earliest Period to About the End of the Fifteenth Century,* London: Walter Scott, 1906.

Rosell, Cayetano, ed., *Cronicas de los Reyes dc Costilla, Vol. I, Madrid, Sucesores de Hernando*, (NBAE 66). 1919.

S. Griswold Morley, *Romance antiguo y verdadero de Alora la bien cercada (ca. 1434), "con la gran artilleria—hecho te habia un portillo."* Spanish Ballads. New York: Henry Holt, 1938.

Sebastian de Covarrubias, *Tesoro de la lengua castellana o espanola*. Madrid, 1611.

Serrano y Sanz, Manuel, *Origenes de la domination espanola en America*, 4 Vols. Vol. I. Madrid, Bailly-Bailliere, 1918.

Smith, Walter George *"Christopher Columbus: An Address Delivered Before the American Catholic Historical Society"*. Records of the American Catholic Historical Society of Philadelphia. (1906).

Soler, Isidro, *Compendio Historico de los Arcabuceros de Madrid*. Madrid, 1795.

Steckel, Captain Johan F., *Haandskydevaabens Bedommelse. Copenhagen, Nordlundes Bogtrykkeri*, 2 vols. 1938-43.

Troche et Luniga, D. Froilan. *El Cazador Gallego con Escopeta y Perro*. Santiago, 1837.

Ulrich Graf Fugger, Von Glött, *The Fuggerei.*

Valencia, de don Juan, *Conde Vdo. de, Catdlogo historico-descriptivo de la Real Armeria de Madrid. Madrid,*. MSS, Archivo General de Palacio, Palacio Real, Madrid. MSS. Archivo General de Simancas, Simancas. MSS. Archivo de Protocolos, Madrid. 1898.

Vicens Vives, Jaime, ed., *Historia social y economica de Espana y America*. Barcelona. Editorial Teide, 1957-59.

Walthoe, John ..., Tho. Wotton ..., Samuel Birt ..., Daniel Browne ..., Thomas Osborn ..., John Shuckburgh ... and Henry Lintot. *A Collection of voyages and travels*. 2. London : Printed by assignment from Messrs. Churchill.

Wey, Gómez Nicolás, *The tropics of empire: Why Columbus sailed south to the Indies*. Cambridge, MA: MIT Press, 2008.

Wilford, John Noble, *The Mysterious History of Columbus: An Exploration of the Man, the Myth, the Legacy,* New York: Alfred A. Knopf, 1991.

Winsor, Justin, *Christopher Columbus and How He Received and Imparted the Spirit of Discovery,* Boston: Houghton Mifflin, (1891).

Zinn, Howard , *A People's History of the United States*, New York, HarperCollins, 2003.

Zolines, D. Francisco, *El Observador en la Diversion de Caza y Escopeta de Piston*. Pamplona, 1830.